WRITING
FOR
TELEVISION

QUANTITY SALES

Most Dell books are available at special quantity discounts when purchased in bulk by corporations, organizations, and special-interest groups. Custom imprinting or excerpting can also be done to fit special needs. For details write: Dell Publishing, 666 Fifth Avenue, New York, NY 10103. Attn.: Special Sales Department.

INDIVIDUAL SALES

Are there any Dell books you want but cannot find in your local stores? If so, you can order them directly from us. You can get any Dell book in print. Simply include the book's title, author, and ISBN number if you have it, along with a check or money order (no cash can be accepted) for the full retail price plus $1.50 to cover shipping and handling. Mail to: Dell Readers Service, P.O. Box 5057, Des Plaines, IL 60017.

WRITING
FOR
TELEVISION

Stuart M. Kaminsky

WITH

Mark Walker

A DELL TRADE PAPERBACK

A DELL TRADE PAPERBACK
Published by
Dell Publishing
a division of
The Bantam Doubleday Dell Publishing Group, Inc.
666 Fifth Avenue
New York, New York 10103

Grateful acknowledgment is made to Harlan Ellison, Bill Nuss, Garry Marshall, Jeff Rice, Bob Shayne, Larry Gelbart, and Garner Simmons for permission to use interviews.

ISBN: 0-440-50025-7

Printed in the United States of America
Published simultaneously in Canada

September 1988

10 9 8 7 6 5 4 3 2 1

MV

NOTES AND THANKS

A brief explanation of the format and style of this book will help you to understand whom you are listening to and why.

The book was written by me with the exception of the chapter on comedy by Mark Walker. Mark, who has taught comedy writing and holds a Ph.D. from Northwestern University, has also contributed to other chapters and was responsible for conducting the interviews with the professional writers from questions that he and I prepared.

The book is written in the first person and reflects my views on writing for television with significant input from the writers who have contributed their experience to making this a practical and honest presentation of what the prospects are for a television writer, what the writer can expect, and what the writer must do.

To these writers and writer/producers who gave their time— Harlan Ellison, Larry Gelbart, Garry Marshall, Bob Shayne, Garner Simmons, Bill Nuss, and Jeff Rice—we give our thanks.

STUART M. KAMINSKY

CONTENTS

FOREWORD by Larry Gelbart   ix

PART ONE

THE MECHANICS OF WRITING FOR TELEVISION

1   What Is in This Book   3
2   Telling Stories for Television   17
3   The Structure of the Tale   30
4   Formats, Spec Scripts, and Proposals   48
5   Creating Characters   82
6   Writing Dialogue   94

PART TWO

GENRES AND FORMS

7   Writing the Police Tale   103
8   Writing Comedy, by Mark Walker   120
9   Writing Made-for-Television Movies and Miniseries   139
10 Writing the Documentary   151

PART THREE

THE BUSINESS OF WRITING FOR TELEVISION

11 Protecting Your Script, Finding a Market and an Agent   163

12 Who Makes the Decisions?   *175*
13 Breaking into the Industry   *198*
    Index   *204*

FOREWORD

By Larry Gelbart

If you know how to read, this book will teach you how to write.

There is a very good reason for this. The author, Stuart Kaminsky, is both a highly skilled professional writer and an experienced teacher who has studied and taught television writing. He and his coauthor, Mark Walker, have created a highly readable and very practical step-by-step guide for the would-be television writer.

Television writing is a profession filled with frustration, heartache, and disappointment. It can also, on occasion, be highly rewarding—both financially and creatively—but those who plunge into a career in television writing without a guide to tell them what to expect will find themselves in trouble. This book provides that guidance.

An important feature of this book is that it draws on the experience of professional writers who speak frankly and illuminatingly on what it means to be a television writer.

However, while this book does contain anecdotal material and does include essential information on the television industry, its strength lies in its concentration on *the* essential element of television writing—writing. You learn how to write for any medium by doing it, not just doing it once or twice but doing it over and over again until you get it right. Many people, unfortunately, never get it right. But if you have the necessary determination, intelligence, and creativity, *Writing for Television* will show you how to get it right.

This book emphasizes the need to work at your craft and provides a series of imaginative and valuable exercises that have been developed and used by the authors from their own experience and that of the professional writers who contributed to this book.

Yes, this book does include formats, information on getting to agents, and other very practical suggestions on how to proceed once you've started to create, but the essence of this book it that it teaches writing.

It's like having a highly skilled professional at your side, a professional who can lead you through, show you the ropes, and tell you what to do next and how to do it. Who could ask for more?

Beverly Hills, California
September 19, 1987

PART
ONE

THE MECHANICS
OF WRITING FOR TELEVISION

These first six chapters contain the nuts and bolts that any beginning writer needs to master in order to write for television:

- What is in this book and how you can use it to your best advantage
- How to tell a story for television
- How to structure your tale professionally
- Information on proper format, on how to write professional spec scripts and proposals
- How to create characters for television
- How to write crisp, professional dialogue

CHAPTER
1

WHAT IS IN THIS BOOK

The first question you should ask yourself is: What do you think this book can do for you?

If you are simply reading the book out of curiosity, the wish to know how television writers work, it should be a quick read, and you will probably learn quite a bit about how television writers think, work, succeed, and fail. If you are considering the possibility of writing for television, this book will give you some insight into what that means, and it should not take you particularly long to make a decision. If, however, you have this book in front of you because you seriously want to learn to write for television, the book should take you some time to get through because it will be of value only to the extent that you do the exercises, do the work indicated. Reading is not enough. This is a book about writing—not about reading. By the time you finish, you should have a relatively thick portfolio of exercises you can refer to in the future as you work on scripts. By all means, keep a notebook in which you can store the writing you do as you go through this book.

While the central concentration of this book is on writing

for television, the ideas and the exercises will be of value to any writer. In fact, most successful writers do not confine themselves to a single medium. Larry Gelbart, for example, has worked in radio, television, film, and theater. Throughout the book, observations by Larry, Harlan Ellison, Garry Marshall, Garner Simmons, Bob Shayne, Jeff Rice, and Bill Nuss, all working television writers, will be included to reinforce, illustrate, and clarify points made about the process.

The Contributors

HARLAN ELLISON: Television credits include writer for *Route 66, The Alfred Hitchcock Hour, Star Trek, The Outer Limits, Burke's Law, The Starlost,* and *Twilight Zone.* He holds the distinct honor of having won the Writers Guild award for Most Outstanding Teleplay four times. He has also won numerous Hugo awards for his fiction, has written many screenplays, and is the author of the highly influential *The Glass Teat: Essays of Opinion on the Subject of Television* and its sequel, *The Other Glass Teat.*

LARRY GELBART: Television credits include executive producer and writer of *M*A*S*H,* creator and writer of *United States,* and writer of the screenplays for the films *The Notorious Landlady; The Wrong Box; Not with My Wife You Don't; Oh God!; Movie, Movie;* and *Tootsie.* He is also author of several plays, including *A Funny Thing Happened on the Way to the Forum* and *Foxy.*

GARRY MARSHALL: Television credits include creator and executive producer of *Happy Days, Laverne and Shirley, Mork and Mindy;* executive producer and writer of *The Odd Couple;* writer for such shows as *The Dick Van Dyke Show, The Danny Thomas Show, I Spy,* and *Love American Style.* He wrote the made-for-television film *Evil Roy Slade* and cowrote the screenplays for the feature films *How Sweet It Is* and *The Grasshopper.* He also directed the feature films *Young Doctors in Love, The Flamingo Kid* (which he also wrote), *Nothing in Common,* and *Overboard.*

BILL NUSS: Television credits include writer for *Good Times, James at 16, Eight Is Enough, Knight Rider, Riptide, The A-Team,* and *21 Jump Street.* He also served as an assistant vice-president for NBC Television and is currently on the staff of Stephen Cannell Productions.

JEFF RICE: Creator and producer of *The Night Stalker* television series; also wrote the story for the pilot and wrote for the series.

ROBERT SHAYNE: Television credits include creator and writer of *Whiz Kids* and *Together.* He wrote the movie-of-the-week *The Return of Sherlock Holmes* and has written episodes for many series, including *Spenser: For Hire, Remington Steele, Simon and Simon, Cover-Up, Tales of the Golden Monkey, Bring 'Em Back Alive, Magnum, P.I., Foul Play, Welcome Back, Kotter,* and *Good Times.*

GARNER SIMMONS: Television credits include writer and story editor on *Falcon Crest,* producer and writer on *Yellow Rose, V, Buck James,* and writer on various series, including *The New Maverick.* He wrote the story and screenplay for the feature film *A Rare Breed,* has been a producer/writer for Aaron Spelling Productions, and is currently with Tri Star Television.

The ideas and exercises in this book are the result of my more than ten years of teaching writing for television, print, film, and theater and an equal number of years of writing for the media. This book is written in the first person. The word *I* will be used and is important. With the exception of one chapter, this book is the view of one writer, an indication of how one writer/educator teaches and writes.

Other writers, even those who have contributed their ideas to this book, might well teach writing for television in a different way. The point is that there is no single way to teach writing. There are many ways, many paths to the goal. You will be taking, trying, testing my path, a path that has worked for me and my students. Hence, the use of *I*.

This doesn't mean that there aren't basic conventions, possibly even rules, you should know. You should know the proper form of a television script. The reason is simple. The form has evolved over the nearly forty years of television scripting, and it is the form that people in the industry can read and understand quickly and efficiently. The form will be given to you. My feeling, however, is that form and formats can be learned quickly and mastered through practice. Practice, in fact, is the essence of learning how to write.

Convention and Invention

Conventions must be learned. As a writer you should know the way things have been done in the past and are being done now. You should know the genres, the lengths, the character types, the stories of the medium.

Garner Simmons on Conventions:

"There are no new ideas under the sun. There are simple variations on old ideas, which sometimes work better than others."

This doesn't mean that you must abide by them, that you can't decide to break conventions, flaunt conventions, attack conventions if you ultimately wish to do so. It is necessary first, however, to know what those conventions are. Put another way, how can you break a rule unless you know what the rule is? How can you alter a convention without knowing the convention? How can you change a genre—the melodrama, police tale, situation comedy, documentary, children's program, etc. —unless you know what that genre is?

Most of you, however, are far from thinking about breaking rules and conventions and changing television. You want to know how to write and how to get in, how to finish that script, get someone to read it, and get it produced. We will discuss these issues, in fact concentrate on them.

Why Do you Want to Write for Television?

- You want to make money.
- You want recognition, possibly even fame.
- You want to share your ideas, your vision with others.
- You want to be seen by others and yourself as a writer.
- You want to show all the people you graduated from high school with that you've made it as a creative individual in a vital, influential medium, even if you never plan to see the people you went to high school with.
- You see being a television writer as a step toward something else—becoming a producer, director, television executive.

It is even possible that many of you want to write simply because you can't help it. You feel you must write and know that you will continue to write even if no one buys, produces, or even reads what you write. It won't make you particularly happy to write without some touchstone of success, but you know you will keep doing it just as you have been since you were ten, twelve, fifteen, or fifty.

Now the reality. There are writers who make a great deal of money writing for television. There aren't many of them, but there is room for more. The competition is great, and it is very difficult to get someone to read your work. The likelihood of your getting rich writing for television is slight. Even if you are successful, which means you start writing for various television series, the pressure is constantly on you to keep it up. You have to prove yourself over and over again with each script, each proposal. Even the most successful television writers run into lean times, periods when the cash runs out or runs down and the MasterCard company must be paid the monthly minimum rather than the entire tab. You could probably make more money as a writer by trying to become a novelist or an insurance underwriter.

By the same token, fame is an unlikely result of writing for television. How many television writers can you name? Now if you, a potential television writer, can't identify more than a few writers, it isn't reasonable to assume that others will either. No, fame is not a likely result of being a television writer.

As for bringing your own ideas to television, that is always a possibility, but it is normally not likely the first time out. As the people in the television industry put it, you must first "pay your dues." You don't begin by creating a proposal and a script for a new television series. In all likelihood, no one will be interested in your new script, your new series, your new special. Producers, most of whom are former writers, have their own ideas, ideas that they have a great deal of difficulty in getting networks to buy. No, your own ideas will probably have to wait. What you will probably have to do for the foreseeable future, possibly for your entire future as a writer, is to write for other people, for series and specials conceived of by others. Your input and your creativity become part of a collaborative creative effort of which the writer is an important part, possibly the most important part. In television, the romantic image of the individual writer is a myth that must be given up if you are to have any real hope for success. Your ego, your belief in yourself, is essential, but it can get in the way. Your work will be revised, changed, turned around by others until it is fused in its final presentation, if you are lucky enough to get that far, with the vision of many other people, including writers, producers, directors, actors, and network executives.

Stephen Cannell became a producer at the age of twenty-four, but he is indeed an exception. Television is, by and large, a popular medium, one in which the writer, if he or she is to be successful, must not only work within a preexisting form or formula but must also be comfortable doing so.

Garner Simmons on Forms:

"The form that [all television writing] fits into has a certain structure that gives satisfaction to the viewer. What you have to do is find new and original ways to rework the material within that structure that surprise and illuminate and fulfill the viewer."

So, what's in it for you? The joy of seeing your thoughts and imagination come to life on the screen—albeit usually a small screen—the possibility of financial reward, and the satisfaction of being able to call yourself a writer. In the television industry, it is frequently said that you are not a writer just because you call yourself a writer. You are a writer when *other* writers call you a writer. As a television writer you also reap the reward of seeing your creative efforts shared by others, the satisfaction of working with others to create a work or works that millions can respond to and enjoy, and the possibility of doing well enough so that you can influence the medium.

A final reward that doesn't even require the success of sale or production is seldom addressed, and it is a satisfaction that many writers seek and experience. When the creative imagination takes over, the process of writing is very much like the process of reading or even watching. Writing becomes a game of creation, an experience that perhaps only a writer can have, of watching, imagining a tale while having the power to alter it. You can make yourself laugh or cry, fearful or frustrated. You can surprise yourself and, when things are going well, finish a twelve-hour day of writing and get up in the morning anxious to get back to the script to find out what will happen to your characters.

And then, when you work in collaboration with others as you must do in television, you have the satisfaction, frustration, and experience of interactive rewriting, polishing, and compromise until your work blends with that of others and appears on the screen.

The reward mixed with frustration comes when you turn on the television set, see your name on the credits, and watch your modified words and ideas unfold in front of you. The next day your friends tell you they liked it or didn't like it, and the day after, having spent hours, weeks, or even months on the project, you have to start again.

What Can and Cannot Be Taught

Before we begin the work, let's address the issue of what can and cannot be taught. I've heard writers in all media declare that writing of any kind cannot be taught, that writing is a talent.

You've either got it or you haven't. Writers who feel this way will usually concede that a few things can be taught, particularly forms and conventions, but that the really essential talents cannot be taught. Usually, writers who believe this have had no formal training in writing. They are partially self-taught, partially taught through formal or informal apprenticeships. Their way worked for them. In most cases, it was a long, frustrating, circuitous route to success and involved a great deal of learning by trial and error. It was their way, but not the only way.

Let's take a brief look at the range of professional opinion on this topic.

Garry Marshall:

"I think film schools or writing schools have two attributes. One is discipline. Two, they force the writer to be around people he may dislike. That's what always happens in the real world. In school you learn to work with people that you don't like. It sounds very simplistic, but it's very true."

Bill Nuss:

"Television writing is a talent. The talent has to be there, and the craft can be taught either in school or in practice."

Larry Gelbart:

"I'm a little disturbed because it seems to me more and more that most preparation for writing for television is other television. I wish that people who would write or would hope to write would know more than just the medium, that they would be able to bring their own experience and their own ideas about life to the screen. Film and television schools just sort of institutionalize what I'm talking about. I still think that it's necessary to know how real people behave, not just how Lucy handles a situation. I think it's important to have your own ideas and your own feelings, your own ideals and not those that you've been watching since the Saturday morning shows when you were a kid."

I believe that most people, perhaps not all, have the imagination to create. What is needed is a way to tap into that imagination, to stimulate and release that imagination—that is what this book can do for you. Incorporated into this book is a series of exercises that can help to free the imagination. There are many things you can learn about structure, character, genres, dialogue. There are tricks, lessons from the past.

Before the imagination can be released, however, you have to have control of language. You have to be able to write. To be a creative writer, a television writer, you must be able to control language. Most people are controlled by language. They are frustrated by being unable to express what they feel, think, hear, believe. They are limited by vocabulary and grammar. You can learn the basics of vocabulary and grammar in school, but until you use them they aren't tools with which you are comfortable. Knowing the rules and conventions is not enough. You have to exercise them and exercise them. The writer, in short, has to write, write, and write until he or she is comfortable with words, until, in fact, the process and rules become automatic. You can begin to hear the voices, imagine the characters interact, but you can't immediately convey what you hear and see to others until you have a command of language and writing that leaves you free of thinking about the process.

I wrote five novels, dozens of short stories, poems, three full-length plays, and a television script before anyone bought a major work of mine. One of those novels, more than three hundred pages long, was completely rewritten three times. That novel has still not been published and, I hope, never will be. I don't think it is much good, but it was part of the process of learning to control language. Analogy: The experienced painter doesn't have to relearn how to paint, how brushes will react, how colors will blend. The painter knows these things. He had to be told about such things when he began either in classes or on apprenticeships or by trial and error. Ultimately, however, the professional painter knows from having painted and painted. The painter simply paints.

The experience of writing can come not only from creative writing but also from any kind of writing that requires control of language. Legal writing, report writing, journalism, and academic writing can all provide this experience.

Feedback and Criticism

A final question: As you go through this book, writing, doing exercises, how will you know what you are learning, how well you are writing? Some people have no one to read their work, either because they are unwilling to risk criticism or because they simply have no one they feel is interested enough in their work to devote the time or effort to it. Others have friends, colleagues, or relatives who will read and respond. If you are really fortunate, you can find a professional who is willing to look at your work and give you an honest response. If you live in a place where short or even long courses are taught by professional writers, take a course or more even if the course does not specifically deal with writing for the media. Be sure, however, that the course involves individual critiquing of what you write in class and, hopefully, what you write outside of class.

At the risk of offending my colleagues at various universities, I think the serious potential writer should be sure that the person teaching the course is a published or produced writer. Check the credits of the teacher. If he or she has no such credits, avoid the course unless you simply need the experience of writing and do not have the discipline to write unless you are in a context that requires you to turn in material.

There are many nonprofessional writers who can, in fact,

teach writing, but the experience of working with others professionally, of coping with producers, networks, other writers, the demands of the medium, is essential to teaching the serious student.

In the absence of such courses, you can get feedback, but not professional advice, from friends and relatives. Take with caution all qualitative comments, both positive and negative, from friends and relatives; they tend to be overly supportive.

Dozens of times beginning writers have submitted stories or scripts for me to read, and when I've indicated that the script or story wasn't very good and needed work, they responded with understandable sensitivity that their friends all liked the story. When I've believed the writers could take it, I've suggested that they get their friends to put up the money and produce their work, because I doubt that a professional producer would be interested.

Sensitivity is understandable, but the writer who is not prepared for rejection and constant criticism and rewriting should stay away from television.

Garry Marshall:

"A lot of times the beginning writer doesn't get the reward of seeing things done in his particular vision. His work is rewritten, pushed around, thrown out, changed, messed up. So, you have to prepare for frustration and not let it get you so depressed that you can't write. You have to be able to write under duress and write tired."

Bob Shayne:

"It's a sad, lonely, unfortunate business, free-lance writing. It's not fun. There's fun in the writing part. The business part is unhappy, distorted. The deck is stacked against the free-lance writer, and it's not a way to make a living. Writing episodes for TV shows is frankly not a career—it's only a way to get into the business."

Harlan Ellison:

"The trick isn't *becoming* a writer. The trick is *staying* a writer."

Enjoying the Process

Let's close on a positive note. This book should be work, but it should also be fun. You should discover things not only about writing and television but also about yourself as a writer. You will discover things you have been doing wrong and things you have been doing right without knowing it. You will learn about deficiencies you didn't know you had, and you'll learn how to overcome them. You'll learn what you can and cannot do in television. If you follow through with all of the exercises and pay attention to the suggestions, you will be far ahead of the competition.

And there is enormous competition. I've known dozens of capable writers who have anticipated the competition and have given up before they started. The odds are against you. They are against me, and they were against all the writers who contributed to this book, but those writers realized that someone has to succeed. Some of them, knowing the odds, decided that it was better to try and possibly fail than never to know if they could have succeeded.

If nothing else, by the end of this book you will know that you are not a likely candidate to become a television writer. That, in fact, can be a very liberating feeling. Instead of going through your life saying "I really wanted to be a television writer," you can discover that television writing or any creative writing at the professional level is simply not for you. Then you can devote your imagination, attention, and energy to something else.

The first thing you need to know is where ideas come from

and how they are turned into proposals and scripts. Then we will go through the steps of writing for television using specific genres of television as case studies. Finally we discuss the business aspects of television, how you can protect your script and get it to those who make the decisions in the industry.

Let's get started.

CHAPTER

2

TELLING STORIES FOR TELEVISION

The proper study of television is television. The first thing you should do as a television writer is to start watching television not as a viewer but as a writer. Start by taking notes, paying attention. Watch with a clock on the television set.

How does a show begin? How are the characters introduced? When is the story line introduced? Is there a second story line? Who is in each scene? How many minutes does it take before the first break—the end of the first act? How does that act end? How many minutes does the second act take? How does that act end? Ask the same questions for the third act. All these considerations are *story* considerations.

Creating the "Problem"

Creating television drama, comic or serious, involves the creation and resolution of problems for the characters. Usually there is one central problem and a central figure who has that problem, as well as a secondary problem that involves one or more of the secondary characters.

Example: On *Valerie,* Valerie leaves her sons at home so she can spend a weekend in Bermuda with her pilot husband. In the snowed-in airport Valerie's purse is stolen, but Valerie is accused of being the purse snatcher. Her problem, obviously, is getting her purse back, proving her innocence, and, if possible, getting to Bermuda. At the same time, her constantly quarreling sons find themselves taking care of a friend's small niece. The boys have tickets to a rock concert. Problem: how to get to the concert while meeting their responsibility for the little girl.

The resolution of the problem need not be perfect. In fact, it normally isn't. In the episode summarized above, Valerie does clear her name and recover her purse, but she doesn't get to Bermuda. The two younger sons do get to the rock concert, but the eldest son stays behind to sit with the little girl. Valerie comes home in the final act to talk to her oldest son. She has learned, through the airport incident, that she is strong enough to handle a crisis. He has learned that there is satisfaction in accepting responsibility. The important point here, however, is that the tale begins with the premise of two problems, problems that involve each member of the cast.

A study of particular shows will indicate the kinds of problems you might want to pursue. The characters themselves exhibit traits, characteristics that suggest problems.

Examples: In *Family Ties* Alex Keaton's pursuit of money and his conservatism constantly come into conflict with his immediate goals—a date with a feminist, a job in his liberal father's television station, a female boss at a bank where Alex wants to work, and so forth. In almost every episode that concentrates on Alex, his conservative self-interest is challenged and he is forced to accept emotional responsibility and/or vulnerability.

In *The Equalizer,* McCall seeks problems by advertising in

the newspaper. However, the trick is to get McCall emotionally involved in the problem. To understand how to do this, a would-be writer must know that McCall is a retired government agent who has been involved in violent actions in the past for which he is seeking a kind of repentance by helping underdogs. McCall has an ex-wife, a son from whom he is somewhat estranged, some friends from his professional days, and many bitter memories. Each problem McCall gets involved with reflects his personal dilemma—a father estranged from his son, a husband having trouble with his wife, a man being pursued by organized crime, a woman with a son who is being terrorized by an ex-husband.

What Makes a Story?

An idea is not a story. It is an idea. A writer is someone who turns ideas into stories. Often someone will approach me saying he has an idea for a television show, novel, play, or film. He says he would like to write the show when he has time. Sometimes such ideas are quite good. Sometimes they are awful. Rarely are they stories. For example, a woman once told me that she had an idea for a television series about a psychic woman she knew. The psychic was a housewife who occasionally was called in by the police to consult on cases. The woman, a librarian, said she had been thinking about writing an episode of the proposed series.

It sounded like a reasonable idea to me. I asked the woman for a story, characters. She had none. On the spot she suggested that there might be a police officer whom the psychic worked with. We might also see her family. As to the story, she thought it might involve finding a missing child since the woman specialized in psychic experiences involving children. Still fine. Still idea. She had fifty or more pages to fill. I asked her if she had thought through the story of the primary problem and if she had a secondary problem. She hadn't and didn't. I asked her how long she had had this idea, and she said she had been thinking about it for a few years.

I suggested that if she didn't have a story after two years of conscious or unconscious fantasy then she probably wouldn't be able to sit down and write a pilot episode. I said, foolishly, that I'd be happy to look at her pilot episode if she ever did write one. The woman responded by saying that she had a better idea. Why didn't I write it and share with her whatever profits might come? This too is something a writer commonly hears. I informed her, again politely, that I had plenty of ideas of my own, that the hard part wasn't the ideas; it was the writing. She was disappointed and walked away, as so many have, convinced that I had been stubborn and grumpy.

Consider this: What is absolutely necessary to tell a story on television? The answer: One person sitting in front of the camera, looking into it and telling the story, or, at base level, the words of the story printed on the screen for you to read.

Now, a script suggesting either of the above is not likely to lead to production because it would not be likely to lead to an audience sufficient to warrant its production. Hold it. I've got an idea for even that minimum that might succeed. How about a series for children in which guest celebrities sit and read bedtime stories? Might make a low-budget cable show. It could come on at 7:00 P.M. and 8:00 P.M. for fifteen minutes. Imagine Charlton Heston reading *The Little Engine That Could,* Stephen King reading *How the Grinch Stole Christmas,* Colleen Dewhurst reading *Are You My Mother?,* or Eddie Murphy reading *Green Eggs and Ham.* Sponsors? Toys, children's books, children's clothing? Not a bad idea, and the scripts write themselves. A producer's idea, not really a writer's.

I can even think of a reason for printing novels or short stories on the screen as a service to the deaf. New stories, expensive new books might be perfect.

So, the minimum might even be commercially possible. But looked at more pragmatically, it takes very little to tell any story. Converting that story into a television pilot or episode involves careful planning, but that planning can be quite clear:

1. Study the genre or series you plan to write in.
2. Outline an episode scene by scene, using two problems, a primary one and a secondary one.
3. Work out scenes in which the problems can be presented in terms of actions and dialogue.
4. Figure out the sequence in which the two problems will be presented and how they relate to each other.
5. Decide on the resolution of the two problems even before you begin writing.
6. Write a treatment of the episode, film, or pilot, estimating how long each scene will take.

A statement frequently made to beginning writers is that they should write from experience, write about things they know. Taken at face value, this is one of the most destructive statements a new writer can hear when trying to come up with stories and plots. Most of us lead lives that simply do not contain the ingredients of high drama. Your life, experience, observations of humanity, dialogue, time, space, and environment are crucial in your writing, but those things that have happened to you are rarely the stuff of television or film narrative.

Frequently heard by writers: Why don't you write a story or television episode based on what happened to us just now? Why don't you write a story about your relationship with your two best friends? Why don't you . . . ?

The answer is simple. No one would be interested. You can use your life experience as a point of departure, take the meaningful incidents in your life and heighten them, underline them with emotion or even understatement, but rarely can you simply relate them.

I have read many a well-written script detailing a thinly disguised love affair of the young writer, many a script about the conflict between a husband and wife, between a son or daughter and his or her parents/parent. I have read many and found few that were the stuff dreams are made of. Reality is the springboard. You have to leave that springboard and soar into the realm of fantasy.

Story and History

In fact, you have no real choice. You have to make decisions about what you will put into your script, which scenes you will show. A literary theorist named Gerard Gennette suggested that when we see a story we are seeing only a small part of the history of that tale, an imagined or real history.

The writer chooses what part of that history we will see and what part we won't see. If the story covers four days and we are dealing with a one-hour script, we see essentially fifty minutes of those days. Actually, we see even less because at the moment we are watching character number one, possibly Alex Keaton in the kitchen, we are not watching one of the absent characters, possibly Mallory in her room or out buying clothes and going to a movie with her boyfriend, Nick.

If history, even imagined history, is a straight line or as many straight lines as there are characters in your television world, you as writer must choose which parts of that history to show. The parts you show are the story.

HISTORY_____

STORY_____

So, obviously, there are many parts of the history that the writer does not choose to show us, and for good reason. The writer makes a decision that those parts of the history we do not see do not relate to the tale he or she is telling, that they are less important to the writer than the incidents, the moments in time, selected.

This can be complicated by the fact that the writer can choose to show two incidents or scenes that are taking place at the same time. At its simplest level, character number one can look at his watch and say "It's nine o'clock. Where the hell is Ralph with the car?" We can then watch character number one go through the scene waiting for Ralph. At the end of the scene we can cut to Ralph in the car talking to Sandy, who says "Ralph, it's almost nine. Jim must be there waiting for us."

The above is not as uncommon as you might think. In fact, it is quite common, though not as underlined as it is in the example. The example actually does something even stranger on the surface. It not only covers the same time in two scenes. The second scene actually begins slightly earlier in time than the scene it follows.

The point? Simple. You have control of time in telling your story. Start at the beginning? Where is the beginning? It's where you want it to be. Remember that horizontal line, that history, is yours to alter, play with, manipulate, tell your story. Don't work for it. Make it work for you.

One way to make it work for you is to know the history, not just the story. Some writers know it unconsciously or move so easily into fantasy that answering questions about the history of their tale and characters is easy. Whether it's easy or difficult, I suggest you work on it, play with it, imagine it.

Story and Character

If you have a script you've written, go back and ask yourself where the other characters are, what they are doing, what scenes they are acting out and whether you can imagine those scenes fitting into your tale even if you don't plan to use them. Robert DeNiro wore the same brand of silk underwear that Al Capone wore while making *The Untouchables*. The underwear never appeared in the film, but it formed part of the history of that character for the actor. He could feel it, call upon it, use it to make that fantasy concrete. And that's exactly what you must do if you are to create the illusion of reality.

Garner Simmons:

"Reality, such as it is, in a world that is totally fantastic and has nothing to do with reality, is based solely upon the creator's ability to see those situations and characters and realize them, first on the page and later on the screen. That comes out of, hopefully, some sort of life experience."

You are creating the illusion of reality, not reality. Your job isn't to make the script real. Your job is to make it plausible, make it seem real, and that takes skill and an understanding of story, character, and dialogue.

Taking Notes

Books on writing are filled with good ideas that beginning writers seldom use. For example, story ideas can come from a variety of sources. You should keep both a notebook (with you at all times to write ideas) and a file (at home). Ideas are fleeting. If you see something that might inspire an idea, write it down or you'll probably lose it.

I took a break from working on this book about an hour ago and came across a piece of information in a newspaper article about Japanese films during World War II. The article observed that Japanese war movies concentrated on the relationship of the

Japanese military personnel to each other. The films rarely showed battles and almost never showed the enemy. The writer of the article suggested that an important reason why the Japanese didn't show the enemy was that there were so few Caucasians in Japan during the war. I was immediately inspired by the article and played ''What if?'' What if the Japanese brought in a group of American or British prisoners of war and forced or convinced them to play American, British, or Australian soldiers in a 1943 war movie? What if they culled their roster to find prisoners who had acting experience? What if some of the actors refused and others agreed? What would it feel like to be in a hostile country and portray yourself and your country as ''the bad guys''? What if one of these ex-prisoners decided to find any prints of the film after the war to destroy the evidence of his collaboration with the enemy? I may never use this. I may use it as the focal point for a script. I may use it only in casual reference (the most likely possibility). The important thing, however, is that it struck me, made me imagine, ask questions, create.

I just pulled my battered notebook from my back pocket. Here are some random entries:

■''Chinese boys and urinal.'' That entry was written a month ago when I was in Vancouver, British Columbia. I was using a regular toilet, and two Chinese boys, about six and eight, who could not speak English came in and began to gesture at me with concern and to act out their belief that I was committing some kind of violation and should be using the urinal. I don't know if I'll ever use the incident. I might use it in altered form, two Chinese kids who can't speak English trying to mime important information for my protagonist.

■''Yukon man who blew himself up with static electricity.'' My wife and I shared a table in a crowded Vancouver outdoor market with a man who had been blown up when the boiler he was carrying exploded from static electricity. He had obviously

been a powerful man but was now undergoing months of reha-
bilitation. I'm not sure what, if anything, I will do with this
either.

■"Idea for a cartoon or bit of dialogue: A maid is being
interviewed. Maid: 'I don't do windows. I don't walk the dog
and I don't do script rewrites.' '' Probably too much an inside
joke, but the idea of a maid refusing to do something you would
never ask her to do is intriguing and might stem from something
odd about her past experience.

■"Hispanic name on a detective agency in East Los Angeles.
The shops, businesses in the area are now Korean and Mexican.
The detective agency is on the second floor of a two-story,
ramshackle walk-up.'' Intriguing. A main character? An epi-
sode involving a Hispanic private eye with a Korean client?
Maybe a cameo or character scene in a series episode?

There are dozens of other entries. Periodically, usually just
before I'm ready to begin a writing project, I sit down, type up
all the notes in my notebook on eight-by-ten-inch sheets, tack
them on the clipboard above my computer, read them through,
and think about them.

I'm amazed at how often I can incorporate my notes and
ideas, how they stand there ready to pick up a scene or a
situation when I don't know where to start it or what to build it
around. My guess is that the mere writing of the note or
observation puts the idea into an unconcious memory bank
where I store it, savor it, consider it, build on it unconsciously
and then have it ready to use or discard.

The file is a bit tougher. Pieces for that come out of newspapers,
magazines, memos written to me, posters I tear from walls. The
idea for one of my novels, which was later turned into a film,
came from a poster in New York, a poster advertising a psychological counseling service by phone. The poster was pointed out
to me by my agent.

I read the newspaper every morning with part of my mind

alert for articles that might yield a situation, an idea, a character, a direction. For example, this morning I pulled two articles,
and there were lots more I could have clipped. One was on
five-foot-three Tyrone Bogues, who has just been drafted by the
Washington Bullets to play basketball in the NBA. Bogues, the
smallest player in the history of the NBA, will be playing on the
same team with seven-foot-six Manute Bol, the tallest player in
the history of the NBA. I'm not sure what, if anything, I'll do
with this article, but the idea intrigues me. It might lead to
nothing more than a passing comment by a character in a script.
It might lead to nothing.

The other article was on Walter Polavchik, the young man
who fought to stay in the U.S. and won when his family moved
back to the Soviet Union. He is now about twenty years old, living
alone, going to college, and working on a book. Lots of possibilities here, such as a series episode about a character like
Walter who is now being stalked, harassed by someone. He
seeks aid from Magnum, the Equalizer, Cagney and Lacey, Alex
Keaton. Who is stalking him? His angry father? The KGB? A
disgruntled parent whose son has abandoned him and who is
projecting anger on Walter? Again, lots of possibilities here.

Some of the finest writers in the history of theater, film, and
television have been terrible at coming up with stories. William
Shakespeare doesn't seem to have had an original story idea in
his life. He picked up old tales, read history books, and applied
his craft to turn the stories into something uniquely his. Will
Shakespeare obviously kept and used a notebook and clipping
file. Closer to home and the present, Raymond Chandler, creator
of Philip Marlowe, author of such films as *Strangers on a Train*
and *The Blue Dahlia,* readily admitted that he couldn't think of
stories. He agonized over story lines, reused material, took
other people's ideas, and turned them into models of the genre
in which he worked.

Research and Playing "What If?"

If you are terrible at coming up with stories, become good at doing the research, reading newspapers and magazines.

And learn to play "What if?" Fantasize, imagine. What if that raggedy-looking guy in the scraggly beard sitting in the doorway was once a million-dollar-a-year television evangelist? What if you opened your door one night when the bell rang and found yourself facing a fully made up clown? What if you were in your basement one night and you heard a digging sound below you? What if your mother called and said she was going to have a baby? What if these things happened to your favorite television characters?

In working out and thinking up stories you've got to shake a great many things you have been taught. Most important, you've got to get rid of the idea that the only important things that happen in your life occur inside and outside your body, that the history of your life, the events that take place each day, is somehow more important than your dreams and imagination. I suggest that your dreams and fantasies are just as real as the food you eat. They take time. They have meaning. You can even make them concrete by turning your imagination into script and story.

L. M. "Kit" Carson, who wrote such films as *Paris, Texas* and *Breathless* and has written for such television series as *The Hitchhiker,* spends a great deal of time sleeping. He has the uncanny ability to remember his dreams vividly, in detail, and he has the talent to convert those dreams into disturbing scripts. Instead of saying that he is going to take a nap in the middle of the day, Kit announces that he is going to work and, in fact, he is.

You can go to work while you work. When I drive, bathe, sit at meetings, or run, I let my imagination loose, work on story ideas, solve plot problems by trying alternatives. It is helpful when driving to keep a small, portable tape recorder handy and put your thoughts on tape as they come up.

Here are two story exercises you should do before you go on to the next chapter. You should do them and continue to do them after you finish reading this book.

E X E R C I S E 1

—Select a television series you like and watch an episode, taking notes to indicate how many scenes there are, who is in each scene, what takes place in each scene. In addition, indicate what the history of that episode is. Does it begin in the evening of day one and end the next night? Does it take a week? There will be times when you can't tell exactly how many days are covered, but you can approximate. Now write an episode covering the same history but using different scenes to tell your story. For example, if an episode of *Newhart* begins with a scene in which Dick and George are trying to put up a moosehead in the lobby of the Stratford Inn, write a scene that takes place at the same time, indicating what Larry, Darryl, and Darryl or Michael and Stephanie are doing. If the *Newhart* episode you watch has a second scene in which we see Michael and Stephanie, then write a scene involving Dick and George.

E X E R C I S E 2

—Select a running character, but not the main character, from a series you like and write a proposal for a spin-off series featuring that character. Include a story outline for the first episode. Example: Prepare a proposal for a series featuring Cliff, the mailman on *Cheers*. You might want to propose two primary locations, Cliff's home and the post office out of which Cliff works. New characters could include Cliff's mother and his coworkers. You might occasionally want to include a character from *Cheers*.

3

THE STRUCTURE OF THE TALE

Structure is not a magic word. It shouldn't be a frightening word. When we talk of structure, we mean the framework on which you have placed your story. We mean the formal elements of the script or story that you can identify and use.

Bill Nuss:

"In all good television writing the story usually comes first, and when the story is all worked out and structured the writer goes back and writes the script. Story structure is very important in both hour-long television and half-hour television. It's being able to see what's happening on the screen and re-creating it. Watch the shows on TV, break them down, and see what the structure is."

Garner Simmons:

"It's very frustrating to find writing that is sometimes pretty interesting in and of itself but knowing that the structure is so far off the mark that if you give this person an assignment you will spend a couple of weeks totally rewriting the script once you get it. You don't want to do that.

"It is much easier from the standpoint of the production company to do a dialogue polish on something that comes in structurally sound but just doesn't quite catch the characters you have in place already. You just need to touch it up here and there. That's much easier than to look at it and realize 'My God, nothing is working. We have to go back to scene one and start over again.' ''

A script is written in a specific number of pages based on the needs of the medium, the number of minutes of airtime to be filled. Script length is a structural consideration. Everything that happens within those pages—when acts begin, when beats come, where emphasis is given, how time and space are handled—is a structural consideration. You as a writer come up with a story idea, and then you place that story within a structure. Aspects of that structure are dictated by the medium, by television, and you should know what those structures and what the conventions of those aspects are.

Garry Marshall:

"Television lends itself to stories that can be interrupted by commercial breaks. Interruptions, breaking the flow, ruin certain stories. These should be made into movies. Stories with episodic kinds of formats, incident stories, seem to work better for television because you can put commercials in easier. This is really a sophisticated concept. The beginning writer might not have any idea how to do this, but after a while you get a sense of it."

Some of the structural aspects are part of the general history of dramatic presentation. How you as writer handle time, space, narrative attribution determines how much control you have over the script, how much control you have over the medium so you can tell the story as you wish it told. The more skillful the writer, the more that writer has control over the structure. The writer may be conscious of that control, and I believe most television writers are very much aware of structure and the ways of controlling it, or the skilled writer may simply control structure at an unconscious level. However, it is very difficult to control what you are not aware of.

It is possible to be a highly skilled, highly successful writer in television even if you are not particularly good at coming up with stories and characters. It is possible if you have a firm control over the structures of the medium.

Harlan Ellison:

"Beginning writers do not understand plot structure. There must be internal logic in a script. Everything pulls everything else along. If you go from point A to point Z, there must be a logical progression."

Bob Shayne:

"Structure is very, very important. Structure is what beginning writers simply do not know. There seem to be two kinds of beginning writers. I've noticed one group who perceive themselves as storytellers and who probably absorb structure rather easily. They can be very successful in television. There is a second kind of writers who are, I think, more talented. This group is wonderful with dialogue, is wonderful at character, and can be very funny. But they tend to have a much, much harder time with structure. To my mind, these are the people with more talent, who are potentially capable of making better movies and better TV shows. But they have a very big struggle in learning how to form something into three acts."

All right, before the word *structure* starts losing its meaning, let's explain.

How Many Pages Do You Need?

Television scripts tend to run about one and a half pages per minute. The reasons are varied, but the most important is that television productions tend to move more quickly than film scripts. There simply isn't time to allow the reactions or postreactions that are common in feature films, even action-filled feature films.

Half-Hour Shows. In half-hour episodes, which run about twenty-eight to thirty-two pages of script, there are normally three acts and, possibly, a tag. By *act* I mean a part of the tale usually separated in time from the other sections of the tale. The final part of the last act or a brief tag or an epilogue might involve a wrap-up, repose, or commentary on what has taken place by the characters, a reorganization of relationships. The first two acts are ten to twelve pages each, and the final act is six to eight pages long. The tag will normally be a page or less.

One-Hour Shows. Normally, in a one-hour television episode, there will be four acts and a tag. Act One and Act Two are approximately twenty-one pages. Act Three is roughly fifteen to twenty pages. Act Four is about ten pages, and the tag, the short narrative section that comments on the concluded action used, is about two to three pages. A one-hour television episode is about sixty-eight to seventy-two pages long.

Television Movies. A two-hour script will normally run one hundred ten to one hundred twenty pages, with the actual screen time being about ninety-five minutes. A cable film will probably run about the same length (even though the cable networks are commercial-free and therefore more flexible, they do generally follow half-hour and one-hour time blocks). Made-for-television movies vary in the number of acts, depending on the kind of story being told. Normally, television movies are divided into seven acts. Obviously, they should not be extremely short (fewer than ten pages), and I suggest that your opening act be at least fifteen minutes, particularly if you are writing a network, as opposed to cable, movie.

Garner Simmons:

"The two-hour feature generally is seen as seven acts. In rough page count it's like a 20-page first act and six 10- to 15-page shorter acts. So, you get a script that is roughly 105 to 110 pages, somewhere in there. Now again, each individual act or segment that falls between the commercial builds to some sort of question or pivotal moment that needs to be resolved as soon as you get back from the commercial.''

One reason for the seven acts is to allow for commercial breaks, but even if there are no commercial breaks it is a good idea to build to mini-climaxes to hold the viewer's attention. It's simply a matter of good storytelling.

Breaking into Acts

Since the hour-long and half-hour forms have significant differences, let's go over breaking into acts for both.

Act One, to use an hour-long show as an example, usually establishes character at the same time as it introduces the problem. In a typical *Magnum P.I.* episode, for example, a young woman arrives in Hawaii expecting to be met at the airport by her father. He doesn't come. She gets in touch with Magnum because she picks his name out of the phone book. The woman wants Magnum to find this father, whom she has not seen in more than twenty years. Magnum agrees but soon finds that someone doesn't want him to find the young woman's father. In fact, someone will engage in violence to keep her from finding her father. Act One takes about one fourth of the script and should end on about page 22 or 24 in a one-hour episode and page 10 or 12 in a half-hour episode.

Act Two usually presents the conflict and action as the characters attempt to deal with the problem. Magnum, with the help of his friends, follows leads, encounters villains, gets shot at, discovers that his client has been taken by the people who are trying to stop Magnum, and ends up facing the woman's father on a beach. The father says he has to shoot Magnum. Act Two ends (on about page 24 for half-hour episode and page 48 for a one-hour episode) with a climax, confrontation, and the promise of resolution, though the promise may appear negative.

Act Three involves the resolution or solution of the problem and covers twenty pages of an hour script and ten pages of a half-hour script. Magnum discovers from the father that he is being sought by a gang of smugglers who believe he has double-crossed them. The father believes Magnum is a hit man hired by the smugglers. Magnum convinces the father that he is not a hired gun and that the two of them must act to save the daughter. The father volunteers to turn himself over to the smugglers, but he and Magnum work out a plan for the father to pretend to turn himself in. They rescue the woman, turn the smugglers over to the police, and father and daughter are reunited.

A tag is an epilogue separated from the last act by a commercial or station break. In the tag, Magnum, the woman, and the father are having a drink. The father tells why he has not seen his daughter in years. Higgins, who has joined them, makes an observation on the importance of family. The somber statement is undercut by a joke, and the episode ends with a freeze frame of everyone laughing.

Remember, the above is an indication of convention. For many producers those conventions have become rules. You may want to vary, change, play with the conventions at some point, but you should first know what they are and how to write within them.

The second plot in the above three acts of a possible *Magnum, P.I.* episode could involve Magnum's promise to Higgins to get a chore done within twenty-four hours.

Let's turn to the half-hour form. Within a short time, probably not more than two pages, you should set your "hook." You should make it very clear whom the script is going to center around for your episode and what the major problem is. Will Ralph Kramden of *The Honeymooners* become rich on the game show? Will Lucy of *I Love Lucy* get a chance to sing at the Tropicana Club? Not long after the hook, introduce the secondary problem revolving around another character. End Act One with a "stinger," a joke that pushes the problem deeper into the show.

Keep both the problems moving along throughout the second act. End Act Two with another stinger, preferably one that puts the problems at crisis pitch, raises questions, keeps the viewer wanting to find out what will happen next. Will Ralph gain any knowledge about music trivia from his ridiculous practice session with Norton? Will Ricky find out about Lucy's plans before she ever reaches the stage?

In Act Three, resolve all the problems you set up. Although Ralph leaves the quiz show as poor as he went in, Alice still loves him. Although Lucy causes a commotion at his club, Ricky still loves her. Add a one-page tag if the show you're writing a spec script for uses one.

The rule on this and most other questions related to style is to watch television with the eye of a writer and not just a viewer to see where these breaks between acts fall and what questions are raised in each act and answered in the next. To do this you should watch television actively, not passively, with notebook and stopwatch at hand.

Beats, Repetition, Tempo

Within each act there must be beats, actions that establish the pace or tempo of the tale. Each scene should end with a question, something to be resolved in the next scene or sequence.

While repetition may be essential to remind the viewer/reader of what is happening and where you are going, each repetition should be brief and reasonable in the context of the scene.

Otherwise it may disturb the tension of the story. So, we know the young woman is looking for her father because she tells Magnum so. Magnum, who hasn't time to do the chore for Higgins, tells Higgins that. Magnum, about to be beaten by the smugglers, explains that he is only looking for the missing father.

Beats are the tempo of a script, the pulse, emphasis, action moments. Writing a script is like writing music. For example, in the *Magnum* story above, we might begin with the arrival of the plane, the young woman getting off, looking for her father, lost, and then there is a beat, a shot of a pair of menacing-looking men watching her. The next scene finds Magnum at home trying to build a ship in a bottle. His voice-over indicates that he is doing this as therapy recommended by a psychologist friend. A delicate final touch is necessary to raise the mast of the small ship. Just as it about to go up, Higgins comes in noisily, breaks Magnum's concentration, ruins the ship. A beat.

As the tale goes on, the beats, the action moments, may come more frequently, building at a climax. You learn to hear, imagine the music, the composition of the script.

This aspect of structure also involves character. Many writers, particularly beginning writers, are uncomfortable dealing with more than two characters in a scene. They write a script in which scene after scene involves two people talking or interacting. The two people may change, but the pace is repeated. Part of the beat and variation of the tale will involve or can involve playing with the number of people in each scene and using different pairings of characters.

So, in the *Magnum* episode proposed, the scene following the scene with Higgins and Magnum might involve a trio of characters, possibly the villains. We can then come back to Magnum and the young woman. Follow this with Magnum getting together with his friends to pursue or find leads to the missing father.

Outlines

Outline, outline, outline. After you've worked out your story, do a scene-by-scene outline of the entire script. Include the location, the characters who will appear in the scene, and a summary of what will take place in that scene. A scene-by-scene outline allows you to get a sense of the beats you can establish and shows you whether you are including sufficient variation in your script and story. Scenes are structural story elements. They can be moved, removed, and altered.

So, your outline might look something like this:

Act One

Scene 1—Airport, Hawaii. The plane arrives. Liz gets off looking around, obviously expecting to be met. No one meets her. She looked disconcerted. She goes to a phone, calls a number. No one answers. A pair of sleazy-looking men watch Liz, follow her. She spots them, is frightened, goes back to the phone booth, checks the phone book for private investigators, finds Magnum.

Scene 2—Magnum's room. He is working on a ship in a bottle. Voice-over explains that he has been advised to do so by a psychologist. Higgins enters, ruins the project, and demands that Magnum perform a chore. The phone rings. It's Liz. Magnum leaves to meet her, leaving an irate Higgins behind.

Treatments

If you have proposed a miniseries or a made-for-television movie, you should prepare a treatment before you move to the scene outline and the script. The scene outline may be seen by no one but you. The treatment can serve not only as an outline for you but as a selling piece for a potential buyer and a rough outline for determining the budget for and needs of the project. It is easier to make changes and compromises at the treatment stage than it is at the scene or script stage. The treatment should be reasonably detailed and should tell the story in broad terms, introducing characters, conflict, problems, story lines, and resolutions.

Here, for example, is the first page of an eight-page treatment for a miniseries I proposed:

OUR FATHER'S HOUSE
A Treatment by Stuart M. Kaminsky

Moving from Russia in the 1890s to Chicago in the 1970s, three generations of the Markovsky family risk their lives to deny their past, gain wealth and power, and earn respect in a country where they feel alienated. Each generation in this family odyssey is doomed to learn painfully that one cannot deny one's immediate or distant past and heritage. The Markovskys wander and survive bloody pogroms in Russia, union gangsterism in New York, and political corruption in Chicago. In a sense, a very real sense, the Markovsky family history parallels the history of twentieth-century America, a history as filled with denial, regret, and the search for identity as that of the Markovskys.

The tale begins at a lavish bar mitzvah party being given on Chicago's West Side in 1943 by Leo Markovsky for his oldest son, Lawrence. Leo, a politician who has succeeded through violence and corruption, has decided to give the party in spite of the fact that he has just received news that his own brother has been killed in a World War II assault in the South Pacific. In the middle of the party, Leo is startled by the appearance of a huge old man who announces that he is Itzhak, brother of Leo's father Abraham. The specter of the old man coupled with the death of his own brother shocks Leo into memories of his father and his past.

At this point, the tale goes back in time to Russia in 1891 and deals with Abraham Markovsky, who stands in a field behind his house in the village of Yekteraslav at the age of twenty. Reviewing his life—through flashback and, possibly, interior monologue, Abraham recalls his failed ambition to become a rabbi, his afternoon affair with his best friend's mother, the tsar's army taking his older brother Itzhak, the madness and death of his father, and the coming of the pogroms to the village. It is the most recent pogrom that has driven Abraham into the cold field. That morning Abraham and his younger brother, Max, killed three Russians who invaded their home. Knowing the soldiers or "The Black Hundred" will come back when the three dead men are missed, Abraham decides to run away to America with his brother Max.

Leaving their mother and sister Bessie with friends in the village, the two brothers make their way west, crossing borders at night, robbing a traveling Russian family in a carriage for money, stealing food. At night Max, who suffered a head wound in the struggle with the Russian soldiers, becomes delirious. With Abraham's help, Max makes it to Danzig, where the two book passage to America with the last of their stolen money. On the boat Max dies from his injuries. Abraham is almost driven mad by his brother's death, his own loneliness, and his guilt at leaving his mother and sister. A young girl who is being sent to her cousin in America helps Abraham, stays with him in the crowd, and promises to marry him in America rather than go to her much older second cousin to whom she has been promised. The two plan to find work in America and pay off the cousin.

When they get to Ellis Island, Abraham is told he cannot enter the country unless he shows that he has $25 or someone who will support him until he gets work. The girl is met by her cousin, who takes her away while Abraham is taken to a holding area for return to Danzig. On the verge of suicide, Abraham is befriended by an Italian youth, Guiliamo Del Vechio, who is also scheduled to be returned to Europe. Abraham vows to himself and God to succeed, to find the girl, to make the world respect him. Guiliamo convinces Abraham that Guiliamo's brother will bail them both out. True to his word, the brother, Allessandro, does bail the two out, though it takes some convincing and a few bribes.

EXERCISE 3

—Write a treatment for the television episode or new series you have been thinking about. Make the treatment for a half-hour episode no more than three pages, the treatment for a one-hour no more than five pages, and the treatment for a made-for-television movie or miniseries no more than twelve pages.

EXERCISE 4

—Using your treatment, write a scene-by-scene outline of the episode, the film, or the first segment of a miniseries.

Identification

The reasons a viewer (or reader of a script for that matter) identifies with a particular character in an entire script or scene by scene is a result of two factors, one of which has little to do with the conscious control of the writer, the other of which is a question of controlling the structure of the story and script.

First, readers/viewers identify with a character because the viewers believe that in some major way that character is like them. The viewers or readers project themselves upon the character. It may be something specific. If you have an Asian mother in your teleplay and the viewer is an Asian mother, identification will take place regardless of what you do with the character. The greater the sympathy and understanding you have for the character, the greater will be the identification, so that not only will the Asian mother identify, but so will most mothers and, possibly, women in general.

It is also possible to find identification with such a character on the basis of profession or situation. If the Asian mother is also an unsuccessful screenwriter, the possibility exists for male viewers to project on and identify with her if they too are unsuccessful screenwriters. If the Asian woman is suffering with a broken arm, it is possible for anyone with a broken arm or those of us who remember what it was like to have a broken arm to identify with her. Remember, identification means empathy. It involves the power of image and action to make the viewer imagine what it would feel like to be that character. Your ability to create vivid characters will to a great extent determine this level of identification.

It is important to remember not to identify solely with a single character in your tale. Too many scripts are destroyed by writers who can identify with their central characters and not with the other characters. As a writer, your task in creating characters is to identify with them all when you write, to imagine what they are feeling, why they are behaving as they are. If you understand them—the good, the bad, the indifferent, the innocent, the heroic—you improve your chances of giving them the illusion of reality and the prospect for identification. Perfect identification within a script involves the viewer's identifying with the entire tale and everyone in it, not just your central character.

Why do we want to control identification? Well, in the case of projection, we want to engage the viewer, bring the viewer into the tale by creating and maintaining the illusion that there is something strongly compelling about these characters that plays a variation on the viewer's own experience, needs, fears, and wishes.

In the case of structural control, the writer wants viewers to follow the path down which the writer wants them to go. The television experience is a fragile one. The screen, normally, is small. The attention of the viewer is not riveted on the screen. There are distractions, interruptions. Television simply does not demand attention the way a novel does or even the way a movie shown in a theater does, or at least used to. Increasingly films are being treated by audiences the way those audiences treat television—without full attention. The challenge to the filmmaker and to the television producer is to find scripts that pull the viewer into attention and identification.

Some of these means of identification are in the hands of the writer. Some of these means of controlling identification through narrative attribution are in the hands of the director. Once again, this has nothing to do with whether a character is good or bad, right or wrong, intelligent or stupid. For example, Hitchcock in *Psycho,* working from a carefully prepared script, manipulated the identification of the audience by aligning us first with Marion (Janet Leigh) and then with the mad killer Norman (Anthony Perkins). This alignment and identification is common in television. *M*A*S*H* presented several episodes in which the camera was the character with whom we were to identify. The television series *ALF* opens with a credit sequence in which we see a home through the eyes of Alf, the alien. However, those are extreme examples of forcing identification.

All right, how do you as a writer control this aspect of the structure of your teleplay? There are several ways.

VOICE-OVER NARRATOR

The easiest way to control identification is through a voice-over narrator. Occasionally a series—*Moonlighting, Kate and Allie*—will do a tour de force episode, essentially a one-person show in which a character tells the story, remembers an incident, comments on his or her relationship to an event or series of events. *Magnum, P.I.* and *Mike Hammer* pick up on the convention of hard-boiled detective novel in which first-person narration and the response of the central figure are central.

However, though it allows the clearest identification, first-person voice-over of a character is seldom used on television. First-person novels are read. First-person narration in television is heard. Television gets the viewers' attention with action and dialogue. Voice-over narration requires the viewer to give primary attention to the audio track of the tale. There's nothing wrong with doing this, but the risk of losing the audience is significant.

There are other problems with writing first-person voice-over narration. Is the viewer to assume that everything he or she sees in this story is the creation or the recollection of the narrator? If that is so, first-person narration limits the scenes and visuals to those in which the narrator takes part or those someone has told to the narrator.

How much narration is necessary to ground the story in the first-person character? How often does that voice have to come back? If the voice is that of a character, are we to question the character's memory, interpretation? Without a narrator we watch a show and assume that what we are seeing is taking place in that imaginary world, but when we have a narrator, are we to question what we are seeing and hearing because it is coming through an involved party, a possibly unreliable party?

Some rather clever pieces of television have played with the idea that the narrator may not always be reliable. Episodes of series in which we see different versions of the same event as they are "told" by various characters point out some of the problems of using a first-person narrator. Sometimes called the Rashomon gimmick, this method of structuring a single tale around multiple viewpoints shows that different characters just might tell vastly different stories even when they are ostensibly relating the same thing.

There is another first-person narrator with whom you won't have this problem, the narrator who does not appear in the tale, is not identified as a character, the narrator identified with the author of the tale. Many documentaries make use of such narration, in which we have an authoritative voice that gives information. Part of the reason for such a narrator in documentaries is to provide information that either cannot be gathered by recording or documenting the subject or would be so difficult, time-consuming, and awkward to present in any other way that narration offers a reasonable alternative. More didactic television documentaries, National Geographic specials, *Wild Kingdom,* Jacques Cousteau specials, and documentaries in which it is essential that someone explain the visuals make frequent use of the unidentified narrator. Use of such a narrator is rare in narrative television. Perhaps the best-known example is *The Twilight Zone,* but even in that series the narrative voice is confined to the introduction and the closing.

So, use of the first-person narrator should be reserved for documentaries, made-for-television movies, and episodes playing with the conventions of the hard-boiled private detective or tour de force comedy or drama.

PERCEPTION

The most direct way of getting the viewer to identify with a character is through perception, grounding your tale or a part of your tale in the memory or fantasy of a specific character. This can come, without voice-over narration, by indicating that we are seeing a dream or fantasy attributed to a specific character. *Moonlighting* has done this several times, and *The Muppet Babies* employed the device regularly. The classical example is *The Wizard of Oz.* As the first-person narration by a character is associated with the hard-boiled detective tale and the first-person narration by a noncharacter is associated with documentaries, perception, dream or reverie, is associated with fantasy.

POINT OF VIEW

Indicating when a shot or a sequence is to be shown from the point of view of a specific character is within the province of the writer. *Point of view* means specifically that the camera is in the position of a specific character, that we are seeing through the eyes of the character. Point of view is not equivalent to first-person narration.

Point of view allows the writer to control identification, but it has to be used quite sparingly for several reasons. First, it is nonconventional. As television viewers, we are accustomed to watching the tale take place. We are not accustomed to being asked to imagine *being* a character. And point of view shots are associated with a specific character by first letting the viewer see the character and that the character is looking at something and then showing us what the character is looking at. Second, the effect of point of view shots is *not* to bring the viewer into closer identification at the psychological level, because the shot is and looks very artificial if not used sparingly. The reasons for this artificiality are many, but a primary one is that the television camera does not see or move like the human eye. Therefore, while the writer can call for point of view, and such shots do control identification, they should not be a primary tool of either the writer or the director.

DIRECTORIAL AND EDITORIAL DECISIONS

Identification can be suggested by a writer but, in fact, is really the decision of the director and editor. The writer can, however, control identification to a great extent through the action described in the script. For example, you can ensure a character's presence by indicating that the character engages in a crucial action even if the character is not speaking. Have the character pick up an object that will figure into the action or have the character react—laughter, anger, etc.—even if he or she is not speaking.

Suggesting the prominence of a character in a scene or shot, based on how important that character is to that scene, is another way the writer can control identification. However, the final decision on where the camera will be placed to reveal that importance, where the character will stand, is up to the director.

The important thing to know before you make decisions about controlling narrative attribution is why you are doing it. What will you accomplish by using, for example, a voice-over narrator? What will you lose? What does it mean to your tale if we are told it is someone's fantasy or dream?

EXERCISE 5

—Take a television episode, possibly one you've already done an exercise with, and imagine presenting that episode with a voice-over narration by one of the characters. Write the opening voice-over. How would the episode and what appeared within it have to be changed to accommodate the voice-over narrator?

4

FORMATS, SPEC SCRIPTS, AND PROPOSALS

Before we get any further into the process of writing, let's address the things every writer interested in television must address. You must know:

1. The proper *format* for a television script;
2. how to prepare a *spec script,* a script written on speculation without an advance or promise of purchase;
3. how to write and present a *proposal* for an episode, a made-for-television film, or a new series.

Format

It might seem reasonable to start this chapter with proposals, but it is unlikely that a proposal will get you started in television. You have to write full-length scripts to show that you can write on that extended level. Submitting story ideas is generally a mistake. Producers don't want story ideas. They usually have enough story ideas. What they need is writers.

Larry Gelbart:

"I think that's a little bit in the area of pie in the sky because I don't think there's a big history of newcomers creating series ideas without having some experience."

Bill Nuss:

"Save your ideas. Take your ideas, put them in a drawer, and save them for when you are an established writer. There are no spec pilots. The networks turn to established writer/producers who have delivered series to create new series and sometimes to screenwriters. The execution of a series is more important than the idea itself. Networks will give out ideas. They'll have areas they want to work with, but what they're really looking for is who is going to deliver that show week to week, who can really execute it. It's not as easy as it seems creating a show. For new writers, you have to learn the show and the form of the shows first. I don't know of anybody who's gotten off a bus and created a show."

Garry Marshall:

"The hardest thing for a beginning writer is to create a series. It usually is a waste of time, because a series original idea is not so much based on what the idea is; it's based on 'Can you write and deliver thirteen more episodes?' If it's a beginning writer, they don't feel they can turn out thirteen more episodes."

Bob Shayne:

"Ideas for new TV series? I think that's a waste of time. I think it's highly presumptuous of a new writer to think that anyone in the TV industry would be interested in his ideas for a new TV series. I think he needs to serve some time working on TV series before (a) he knows what constitutes a good and commercial and workable series and (b) he has a track record that will impress TV executives enough for them to be interested in his ideas for series."

So, pick out a series, preferably one that is likely to be around for a while, and prepare a script. Better yet, write scripts for several series, both hour-long and half-hour.

When the script is written—and don't write it until you finish this book—there are several ways to get it read by someone in the industry. One is to take a course with a writer who has an agent and might be willing to show the script to the agent. Scripts for series are also occasionally submitted by network executives in charge of the series. Network executives tend to change quickly. The most efficient way to find out whom to submit your script to is to call or write to the network and ask. The same is true of the production company. Often, however, production companies are reluctant to read unsolicited scripts submitted for their series out of fear that they will later be accused of stealing the ideas of a free-lance writer and be subject to a lawsuit.

In truth, it is rare that a script or idea from a new writer is stolen. The reasons are many. First, most producers are honest, either by conviction or because it pays to be so. A producer loses his reputation quickly by appropriating the ideas of others. More important, perhaps, is that it is far easier to pay the new writer for his work than to risk the problems of accusation of theft. The problem, however, is for the beginning writer only. The established writer is protected by his agent and by the Writers Guild. Even non–guild members, however, can register their work with the guild. The process is relatively simple. See Chapter Eleven.

Remember, producers are not really looking for ideas, at least not your ideas. They are looking for writers who will be able to turn their ideas into finished stories and scripts. Before you can get a producer to look at your proposals or ideas, therefore, you must convince the producer that you are a writer. You do that by having credits.

This means, simply, that you have to write. I have been amazed, as a teacher of writing, at how many people want to be writers and how few actually want to write. Writing is hard. Doing the exercises and following the recommendations in this book is not easy. It can be fun. It can be rewarding. But only a few will find it easy.

So, the first thing you must do is write.

And you must write in the form that television people—producers, directors, writers, executives, actors, crew, etc.—understand. A television script is both a guide to visual/verbal thinking and a blueprint for people to understand what they are going to need and to do. Many producers will thumb through a script and, without reading it, know if they are dealing with a professional or an amateur. One giveaway of the amateur is long—a quarter of a page or longer—passages of dialogue by a single character. Occasionally, a long passage is essential, might even be arresting, but including more than one or two in a typical television script is potentially dangerous. Producers will also thumb through to see if there are long—half a page or longer—passages of dialogue without action. Television involves an interplay of dialogue and action. Normally if one has to suffer, it will be the dialogue, but there is no reason why anything has to suffer. Action can take place during dialogue. For example, almost any episode of *M*A*S*H* or *Cagney & Lacey* will be heavily oriented toward dialogue, but the dialogue is in the context of action. That is, something is happening while the characters are talking, and the action is not, or shouldn't be, intended simply to keep them moving. The action is part of the tale being told. So, Hawkeye and Frank or Charles can be exchanging barbs for three quarters of a page, but they are doing so while they are in the operating room dealing with a new influx of wounded, and their interchange also will reveal something about the central issue of that episode—Hawkeye's weariness, Colonel Potter's concern about his wife, and the like.

I've mentioned some general things about format. Let's take a closer look at television format examples on pages 55, 56, 57, and 60 to illustrate how your script should look when you write it and why it should look that way.

The first page should give the title of the series, if you are doing a series episode, centered about a third down the page, and should be capitalized and underlined. Below this, in quotes, should be the title of the individual episode. About six spaces lower should be "Written by" with your name centered below. In the lower right-hand corner, also capitalized and underlined, should be the number of the draft, which version this script is, and below that the date you completed that draft. A first draft, therefore, would simply state *FIRST DRAFT,* a second version or draft would state *SECOND DRAFT,* and a final draft would read *FINAL DRAFT.*

Your second page should list the characters who will be included in the episode you have written. This includes regular cast members, guests (nonrecurring characters with speaking roles, even a single word), and nonspeaking characters and extras. List the characters. Do not list the actors, even the regular cast members. The third page should include the sets and list them by interior and exterior. The reason for the cast list and location list is simple. The producer wants to know how much this episode will cost and whether you have included everything the producer believes is essential. For example, many shows require that members of the continuing cast appear in every episode.

The production manager will want to know how many locations will be needed outside the studio and how much can be shot on standing sets so that the manager can estimate the shooting time of the episode. Television episodes shoot on tight schedules. Most producers are willing to, perhaps even anxious to, move to locations or deal with out-of-the-ordinary sets, because they add the illusion of "production value," which simply means the producer wants the episode to look as if it has some money sunk into it.

Going overboard in this regard, though—making unreasonable suggestions as to locations, sets, and cast—can earn you the wrath of a producer. You should temper your suggestions, therefore, with a bit of an eye to economic feasibility, especially in half-hour comedy.

Garry Marshall:

"There are a lot of limits, and that's what the beginning writer doesn't seem to know, and that's where he messes up. He's got to find a way, by reading scripts or watching the show a few times before he attempts it. It takes basic intelligence to see what a show is doing. Also, in my opinion, many of the people submitting scripts are rather dumb, because they'll watch a show like *The Odd Couple* or a Lucy show, and they'll see it's all done in two sets. Then they submit a script where Lucy goes up in a hot air balloon. Don't they understand that there are considerations in production?"

Larry Gelbart:

"If it's a half-hour series, then obviously you're obliged to use the existing sets, because it's just not financially profitable to indicate that your characters are all over the place. It can't be done. Those sets are as much a part of the series as the actors are."

Bill Nuss:

"There should be limitations on both characters and locations. In a sitcom, there are usually a few guest characters, four or five. In an hour-long show, up to maybe a dozen, sometimes fifteen. If a character is a real small part, you have to decide whether the character needs to exist or not. An actress with one or two lines costs quite a bit of money. Locations are usually ganged, if possible. That's when you go back to a place a couple of times. You can't have twenty-seven scenes in twenty-seven different locations. That would be impossible to shoot in seven or eight days."

As you move up the scale in terms of cost, from the half-hour show to more costly forms of television, dramas, movies, and miniseries, you can be more adventurous. Still, you will find limitations in these forms as well.

Bob Shayne:

"There's a trick that applies especially to one-hour drama, which is to try to reuse sets and locations. You may use nine, ten, eleven different locations in the first half of an hour show, and that may be all right. But, it's going to be all right only if you can reuse five, six, seven of those in the second half. If you are going to use nine, ten, eleven new ones in the second half, it's going to be impossible on a series budget."

Larry Gelbart:

"The same is true of course for television movies. While their budgets are now quite, quite high, still you're not writing as you would for motion pictures. You're hoping that your work will get done, and it's never going to get done if it's not realistic in terms of where your scripts are set and the number of people playing in them."

Another working professional offers a positive, somewhat dissenting note:

Garner Simmons:

"Very little is impossible. What you have to do is simply write it the best way you see it, and they will tell you what they don't like. You will have a chance to rewrite it at least once, usually, unless you are so far off the mark that they just don't want to deal with you again. It is more important that you get down on paper what you believe in."

Other kinds of information may be included, such as the chronology, the scenes that cover individual days in the story, but the above are the essential cover pages.

Sample cover page:

<u>RIPTIDE</u>

"Baxter and Boz"

Written by
Bill Nuss

<u>FIRST DRAFT</u>
November 10, 1984

Example of cast page:

THE A-TEAM

"LEASE WITH AN OPTION TO DIE"

CAST

JOHN "HANNIBAL" SMITH
TEMPLETON PECK (FACEMAN)
B. A. BARACUS
HOWLING MAD MURDOCK

MRS. BARACUS
KAREN MESSING
RICO
LUIS ALVEREZ
DAVE PLOUT
PHILLIP CARTER
HILDY HENDERSON
HARVEY BRUCKNER

HIRSCH
LANG
RALPH
DOROTHY
LITTLE TOMMY
GOON
MAYOR

CATERERS
WORKMEN
TENANTS
SLEAZEBALLS
PARTY GUESTS
CHAUFFEUR

Example of location page:

A-TEAM

"LEASE WITH AN OPTION TO DIE"

SETS

EXTERIORS

700 FOSTER
  FRONT STEPS
  SIDEWALK
  STREET
PARK
SMALL AIRPORT RUNWAY
LEXINGTON SQUARE
CARTER PLAZA
  ROOF
CHICAGO STREETS

INTERIORS

A-TEAM VAN
PRIVATE JET
  COCKPIT
  CABIN
700 FOSTER
  HALLWAY
  ROOF
  BASEMENT
  LAUNDRY ROOM
ALVEREZ APARTMENT
MRS. BARACUS'S APARTMENT
  LIVING ROOM
  DINING ROOM
  KITCHEN
  BATHROOM
LEXINGTON SQUARE
  HALLWAY
  PLOUT'S OUTER OFFICE
  PLOUT'S OFFICE
CARTER PLAZA
  GARAGE
  VALET STAND
  CARTER'S RECEPTION AREA
  CARTER'S SUITE
  BASEMENT
HALL OF RECORDS

As for the body of the script, the description and dialogue, remember that you are writing scenes, not individual shots. Don't worry about long shots, medium shots, and close-ups. Don't worry about over-the-shoulder shots or two-shots. Simply write the scene. If you believe it is essential to have a different visual perspective for a particular shot or action, simply write "Angle" (see page 60) and let the director decide what angle, if any, he or she would like to move to.

Bill Nuss:

"Calling for shots in an hour-long script should mostly be for pointing up something dramatic that you don't want the reader to miss. In that case, you do call a specific shot. You are not directing it; you're writing it."

Larry Gelbart:

"I wouldn't put any camera directions in a first script at all. They're ignored by the readers at production companies totally. It's just not a concern if people can indicate good camera angles."

Films and television are shot by shooting a master shot, the main shot of a scene that takes in all the action from one camera. After the master shot of the entire scene is finished, the director goes back and shoots pieces, actions, reactions, even phrases or individual words. The editor later makes decisions on how much of the master shot to use and which additional shots to add and where they should be. Sometimes the producer gets involved in these decisions. Sometimes, though more rarely on television, the director gets to give input on which shots will be included. Rarely, if ever, is the writer asked for his opinion on this.

Even television shot on tape, primarily half-hour comedy, which may rely less on the master shot and more on decisions by the director while the episode is being taped and afterward, involves the idea that the script is shot by scenes and not in terms of individual shots. Too many first scripts are slowed down, even destroyed, by a writer's including too many orders and suggestions about shots, lighting, and camera position. Leave those to the director and the crew and concentrate on the script.

Garner Simmons:

"What you want to do is to adhere primarily to fairly simple camera directions or stage directions. If you elaborate too much, it's just going to be ignored by the director anyway. Beyond that, in some cases you can alienate the reader. If it gets too convoluted, if you're explaining too much, the reader will sometimes become uncomfortable."

Garry Marshall:

"I would say avoid all the technical jargon. Just write the story and the dialogue. Technical jargon has nothing to do with writing. Writing has to do with emotion, laughter, goodness, storytelling. It has nothing to do with panning."

Jeff Rice:

"Keep it simple. FADE IN. EXTERIOR (or INTERIOR), DAY (or NIGHT). Set the scene in master shot form. Maybe, once in a while, you can indicate ON (and the subject of the shot) for a two-shot or one-shot. And then write your dialogue and end up with FADE OUT. Forget things like CUT TO and WHIP PAN and DOLLY and TILT and DISSOLVE TO and all the good stuff you see in your head that you are so dearly tempted to put into that script."

Let's look at the sample script page, which begins Act Two. The sample page begins with FADE IN. A fade-in is a technique that begins with a black screen that fades to reveal the image. This can be quite rapid, a matter of little more than a second or two. Fade-ins indicate a time separation from the

Example of script from a television episode.*

ACT TWO

FADE IN

32 EXT. FRONT STOOP—ALVEREZ AND THE GOONS—NIGHT

They come out the front door laughing and climb into a van parked across the street.

33 ANGLE—SEDAN

B.A. behind the wheel, Face riding Shotgun. They pull out after the van, following at a safe distance. Face picks up the walkie-talkie.

FACE
Tenant two to tenant one ...
they're on the move.

34 EXT. VARIOUS STREETS—NIGHT

B.A. and Face trail the van through the streets of Chicago. The van pulls up in front of Lexington Square, a modern office building. B.A. and Face park across the street.

35 EXT. LEXINGTON SQUARE—ALVEREZ & GOONS

disappear inside the building.

FACE
Give me five minutes.

Face gets out and scampers across the street and inside the building.

36 INT. LEXINGTON SQUARE—OFFICE BUILDING

Alverez and the Goons look out of place in this sleek building. They head into the office of Lexington Management, on the ground floor.

CONTINUED

---

*Documentaries usually follow a different type of format, "European format," which is discussed in Chapter Ten.

previous action. A dissolve, similar to a fade-in but suggesting movement in both time and space, is the gradual (again sometimes rapid) overlapping of two separate images with the second replacing the first. Simply put, you see an image on the screen and another image, the next shot, appears over it. The image from the first scene disappears to be replaced by the next shot.

Each separate shot is numbered. Note the numbers 32 through 36 on the page. Shots involve a new position, a necessary new placement of the camera. They must be numbered for many reasons, one of which is that the people who shoot your script need to know how many different camera setups they will need and how much time it will take to move to and shoot at a location.

You must indicate whether each shot in your script is interior (inside) or exterior (outdoors). Again, the people who will shoot your script have to know what lighting and equipment they will need. Shooting outdoors is quite different from shooting indoors. Both have advantages. Both have problems. Shot 32 is EXT., an abbreviation for *exterior*. INT., an abbreviation for interior, appears in shot 36.

Following the indication of whether the shot is interior or exterior is an indication of location, where the shot takes place. In shot 32 it is the FRONT STOOP. Sometimes the line in capitals indicating the shot will include the people in the shot. As you will note, you should also include in that top line whether the shot is NIGHT or DAY.

Below the all-caps line that indicates time and location, a line is skipped, and with the margin lined up at the left with the information line you provide an essential description of the shot. Use all caps here for the first mention of a character's name, the regular capitalization for names thereafter. The art of description is to have no art, to avoid calling attention to what you have written. Remember that you are writing to give information to director, actors, crew. You are not writing to entertain a reader. Include only what can be seen and keep it as brief and concise as possible. Do not, as a rule, include descriptions or indications of how a character feels or thinks; be sure that the description you give can be turned into action.

For example, if you write "James, filled with remorse over what he has done, decides to confront Davis and settle the matter," how does the actor who plays James show that he is filled with remorse? How do we know that he has decided to confront Davis and that he means to settle the matter? We don't. When you ascribe an emotion or a response to a character, try standing in front of a mirror and projecting that emotion or response. What does it look like?

The trick, actually the art, of television script writing is to show through action and indicate through words what you want to convey.

How about this instead?

James clenches his teeth and looks back. He shakes off the tears that may be coming and looks at the door to Davis's office. He takes a deep breath, wipes his face with the back of his hand, opens the door, and steps in.

Not perfect, but better. It gives the actor and director specific information on how they can perform the shot. They may reject what you have said, may come up with a better—or at least different—idea, but they know what you want. It isn't vague, and it is brief.

Generally, however, if your description and story are clear, you need very little description of character reactions. You need only indicate what is happening physically.

The dialogue, which comes next, begins with the name of the character who is speaking centered and in caps.

Below the identification of the character we have the actual dialogue centered and indented. We'll discuss more about dialogue in Chapter Six, but for now remember that dialogue segments should be brief. Rarely will a character make a speech of more than one third of a page in a television episode. Even one third of a page is long for television.

If you must give indications to an actor about how his or her character is to act or feel, you can do so by putting the direction in parenthesis below the character's name:

JAMES
(angrily)

That is it, Davis.

Note that I said "if you must." My inclination is *never* to give such direction. Your intention should be clear to the actor if you've written the script clearly.

You can also include indications of reaction or feeling within the description before the character speaks, but once again, I suggest you minimize such direction. If you've done your job well, you don't have to indicate feelings. They'll be clear from the action and the dialogue.

Finally, at the bottom of the page, to the right, indicate in all caps that the script is CONTINUED on the next page. When you reach the end of an act, make a statement, centered on the page, that the act is over:

END OF ACT ONE

Always begin the next act on a new page. On the final page, centered and probably underlined, write THE END.

Format is essentially that simple. Too many beginning writers worry far too much about form. The form can be learned in minutes. The trick is to understand why that form exists and how you can create within it. You must learn to think in that format, to imagine what you have written being turned into image, action, and dialogue, and you must get to the point where everything you write can be clearly envisioned within that format by someone else who is reading it.

Spec Scripts

A spec script is one written on speculation and submitted to an agent or producer, not for a fee in the great majority of cases but as a sample of your writing ability. If you are a beginner trying to break into the industry at a national or network level, you should begin by writing spec scripts rather than original scripts for new or proposed series. Simply put, this means that you should select an ongoing series, preferably one that is likely to last a few more seasons, and after studying the series write a script from your own story.

Jeff Rice:

"This is a situation where you're damned if you do and damned if you don't. Writing scripts on spec is a fast road to bankruptcy because, aside from the occasional miracle, they won't be sold. On the other hand, if you do not write scripts on spec, you will have nothing to show anyone."

Studying the series means understanding each running character—major and minor—and the emphasis each character gets in an episode, determining the genres or kinds of stories told, and anticipating where the series is going. It is normally a good idea in writing a spec script not to do anything radically new, not to change the story line or make a major adjustment in a character that would alter that character for the remainder of the series. For example, don't marry off a running character in a spec script. Your job in writing a spec script is to indicate to whoever will read it that you understand the series, are a professional writer, and are capable of writing not only for that specific series but within that genre—comedy, mystery, melo-drama, or whatever the case may be.

Bill Nuss:

"In writing the script, the important thing is to write exactly in the style of the show in terms of tone or comedy or type of humor. Jokes in *Laverne and Shirley* are far different from those in *Cheers*, and the ones in *Cheers* are far different from those in *Night Court*. The producers want to be able to see if you can hear that show and write those characters. 'Can you write the way Sam and Diane speak?'

"Toward that end, the biggest hint I can give to anyone writing a spec script is to choose a story that is taken from characters in the existing series. In other words, don't do Sam's crazy Uncle Charlie comes to visit the bar in *Cheers*, because then you are writing crazy Uncle Charlie, whom we don't know, and the jokes are going to ride with him rather than riding with the show's characters."

In all likelihood, the spec script you write will never be used. You are not selling the specific script. You are selling yourself as a writer.

Bob Shayne:

"The only time that I would have to get interested in a beginning writer is if he was written a script that just knocks me out of my socks. I have no way of knowing whether a beginning writer can write unless I read his script."

If you are phenomenally lucky, your spec script might actually make it into production.

Garner Simmons:

"What you wind up getting, you hope, is a chance to come in and pitch your idea. Television shows generally do not buy scripts done on spec. Rarely does somebody write a spec script and turn it in and have everybody fall on the floor and say, 'Boy we want to do this one!'"

If you are reasonably lucky, your spec script will indicate to a producer or story editor that you might be a good choice to write an episode for the series. Should that be the case, you might be called in and given an entirely different story to write.

Another possible outcome, and one that happens frequently, is that the producer or story editor for the spec series will send your script on to someone on another series for which he thinks you are better suited. It might be that the series you have written for doesn't need any more writers or any more scripts but the person who reads your script knows of an ongoing or a new series that is looking for writers. Often, if you are lucky again, the story you have written can be adapted for a series other than the one for which you have written.

You don't necessarily have to send your spec to the producers of the same show you have written. You can also send it to a show of the same genre. Let's illustrate with an example from a professional TV writer who favors a slightly different approach.

Garner Simmons:

"If you write a show for *Spenser: For Hire*, clearly you're going to spend most of your time writing for the characters that have already been created by the staff. Don't send it to *Spenser: For Hire*. Send it to *Scarecrow and Mrs. King*. Send it to *The Equalizer* or any one of the number of that kind of detective shows. The people who write on the staff of *Spenser: For Hire* will automatically be predisposed to who these characters are and what their show is like, and they will nitpick your show to death in all probability. There's an advantage to doing it that way: if you send it to somebody else, they have no preconceptions at all about what the show is. They just know they need writers who can put a story together and know how characters work."

It is also important to write more than one spec script and, probably, to write scripts in various genres. The more scripts you write—assuming that they are professionally written—the more likely you are to catch someone's attention.

Bob Shayne:

"You can't be stingy. You need various kinds of spec scripts to get various kinds of jobs. You need to sit down and write a spec movie. You need to write two or three spec episodes of the kinds of shows you want to write for."

Another advantage of writing a number of spec scripts is that it demonstrates to agents and producers that you are capable of writing quickly and that you are flexible, both of which are of great importance in television. It is important in writing a spec script, or any television script, not to fall in love with your words or ideas. Television eats ideas. Write your spec script, send it on, and then go onto the next project.

Garry Marshall:

"The reason people don't want to do spec scripts is they're afraid they'll blow a good idea for free. But if you have only one good idea, you should go into another field. To be writing for television, you have to turn out a number of scripts. Fine writing in television is not applauded as much as writing consistency. Writing every week is what's sought after. If you want to do one wonderful script, you should write a movie of the week. I think Jerry Belson and I hold the record for most scripts in one season, which was thirty-three half-hour scripts. We made our reputation not so much on the fact that they were wonderful scripts but on the fact that there were so many of them."

If you write a spec script and the series you have written for is canceled, your script is not necessarily dead. It is still worth showing. The ideal, however, is to rewrite the script to fit another series.

Initiative and aggression are important factors. I've known writers who have sold scripts to a new series by watching the promotional pieces, reading about the series in *Variety* or *Hollywood Reporter,* studying the past work of the stars, and writing the spec script even before an episode has been aired. It's a gamble, but a gamble sometimes pays off.

Almost every professional film or television writer will tell you the same story. I'll tell it. Some of the best writing I have done for film and television has never been produced and probably never will be. A producer may buy it and sit on it. A network may cancel a series owning the script you wrote, which has never been produced. But some of that unproduced work was seen by people who hired me to write for something else they were doing or planned to do.

I'd also suggest that you write spec scripts for series you like. You might as well enjoy what you are doing. There may come a time when you are hired to write for a series you don't particularly like. Most professionals will do it and do their best, but until you are hired for a particular series, write for something you enjoy.

Chapter Thirteen will tell you how to get someone to look at your spec scripts.

Proposals

Keep this in mind when you come up with proposals or ideas for television shows: Your chances of getting a proposal accepted for a new series, a special, a movie-of-the-week, or a documentary are slim if you are a beginner. They are slim even if you are an established professional, but that's no reason to give up.

The odds are bad, but someone has to succeed, and it might as well be you. I've known many talented students who have given up without trying simply because they knew the odds were against them.

Whatever you are proposing—a movie-of-the-week, a new series, a documentary, a special—and whether you are proposing it to a producer, an actor, an agent, or a network, there are some simple "rules" to follow. The word *rules* is in quotation marks because the truth is there are no rules. There are ways I work that have worked for me and ways other people have worked that have worked for them. So, the "rules" here are really suggestions.

Keep it brief. The proposal itself should be no more than six to twelve pages. The proposal should have a one-page cover summary sheet. If you want to include a full-blown treatment—maybe ten pages for a half-hour series, fifteen for an hour-long series, and twenty or twenty-five pages for a two-hour show—make the treatment itself clearly and distinctly separate from the rest of the proposal. An ideal package proposal would include a one-page summary, a six-plus-page proposal, a treatment, and, if you really want to be ambitious, a script. If your script is finished and in good shape, you can skip the treatment. All of this should be neatly packaged and bound with a contents sheet and your name on every page and your address on the cover page, which will include the title of your proposed project.

In your one-page summary, hit the highlights of your show or series. For example, here is a one-page summary for a television series based on a series of novels I have written.

The Toby Peters series would combine several areas of popular interest—the private detective genre, comedy, and nostalgia.

Set in Los Angeles in the 1940s, the series involves Toby Peters, a fifty-year-old down-and-out private detective, with a different celebrity client each week, most of them movie personalities, some of them from the world of theater, sports, and even politics. Story outlines are ready for individual episodes featuring Errol Flynn, Judy Garland, Bela Lugosi, Eleanor Roosevelt, Joe Louis, Gary Cooper, John Wayne, Mae West, Emmett Kelly, Howard Hughes, Albert Einstein, and the Marx Brothers with cameo appearances by Buster Keaton, Charlie Chaplin, William Faulkner, Raymond Chandler, Paul Robeson, and many others.

One possibility: The celebrity clients could be played by

contemporary celebrities who might identify with or be identified with that historical character. For example: Clint Eastwood playing Gary Cooper, Liza Minnelli playing Judy Garland, Burt Reynolds playing Errol Flynn, Billy Crystal playing Charlie Chaplin, James Earl Jones playing Paul Robeson.

Running characters for the series include Toby Peters; his best friend Gunther Wherthman, a three-foot-tall Swiss translator who appeared as an extra in The Wizard of Oz; Sheldon Minck, the myopic and far from sanitary dentist with whom Toby shares office space in the seamy Farraday Building; Jeremy Butler, the massive ex-wrestler, part-time poet, and landlord of the Farraday; Mrs. Plaut, Toby's ancient and feisty landlady who involves the frenzied Toby in everything from collecting scrap rubber for the war effort to editing the Plaut family history; and Phil Pevsner, Toby's police captain brother whose love-hate relationship with Toby complicates almost every case with which Toby gets involved.

Murder, blackmail, and comic mayhem are set against the studios, the beaches, the desert, and the constant anxiety over World War II, which dominates the conversation, radio reports, and newspapers.

Each episode would end, as the novels do, with a teaser about the next celebrity client in the form of a phone message from Albert Einstein or a note from John Wayne's secretary.

The six-page (or more) proposal that would follow would briefly outline the highlights of particular episodes. For example:

Toby, who is down to his final clean shirt and his last two dollars for his favorite meal of tacos and Pepsi, looks up from the cluttered desk of his cubbyhole office in the Farraday and sees Eleanor Roosevelt come in lugging two shopping bags. The president's wife tells the detective that she believes FDR's dog Fala has been kidnapped and an impostor dog placed in the White House. Toby's task: to locate the real Fala before the president finds out he is missing.

In the course of tracking down the missing dog, Toby

enlists the aid of Jeremy Butler and Gunther Wherthman and follows a trail from an animal hospital to a public rally for a crackpot political group called The New Whigs to an old warehouse where Buster Keaton is making a two-reel comedy.

The proposal would include additional information on the running characters:

Before becoming a private detective, Toby Peters served unsuccessful terms as a Glendale cop and as a security guard at Warner Brothers, where he was fired for punching a loudmouthed cowboy star he was supposed to be protecting at a movie premiere. Toby's ex-wife, Anne, left our hero when it was obvious to her that he would never grow up and would probably never be able to earn a living. Toby, however, has never given up hope of getting back together with Anne, though he has never shown any willingness to change his ways.

Toby's father was a grocer in Glendale. Toby's mother died when he was a child. When Phil went into the army in World War I, Toby helped out in the family grocery. Toby and Phil's father died shortly after the war. Phil, who was wounded, became a cop, and so did Toby, who wanted to prove something to himself and his ill-tempered older brother.

Phil is married; has two sons and a baby daughter, Nate, Dave, and Lucy; a wife, Ruth; and a mortgage he can't keep up with.

Toby, who lives marginally at best, lives in Mrs. Plaut's boardinghouse and operates out of a closet-sized office just beyond the offices of Sheldon Minck, D.D.S. Although Toby has a reputation for discretion, which earns him the occasional celebrity client with a secret, he frequently has to take odd jobs as a fill-in hotel house detective or a defense plant security guard to pay his rent and keep him supplied with cereal, Pepsi, and tacos, all of which he lives on.

In spite of worrying about where his next pair of socks is coming from and whether his bad luck will give out without warning, Toby enjoys his life as long as he doesn't pause long enough to really think about it.

   If you include a treatment, the treatment would cover the story of one proposed episode, probably the first in the series. Often, as I indicated earlier, the first episode of a dramatic series will be a two-hour movie-of-the-week rather than an episode. The reason is clear. The movie can stand on its own to fill a movie time slot. Reaction to the movie can then be judged—in terms of ratings, reviews, word of mouth—to determine whether the idea should go to the series stage. If the decision is negative, the network has lost little and has a two-hour movie for syndication or to fill a late-night rerun slot.

   Here is an example of a proposal letter to a producer. It's an actual letter of mine, the second in a series of letters after several phone conversations. The producer had the idea, a made-for-television movie inspired by the 1960 theatrical film *The List of Adrian Messenger,* a mystery/thriller that involved a criminal who specialized in disguises and included the gimmick of having guest stars appear in cameo appearances in disguise so that the audience would not only watch the detective solve the crime but also have a puzzle of their own to solve, which characters were famous actors in disguise. I suggested a story line that the producer was not wild about. One of the things I had done in the original story line was to introduce two characters who might form the basis for a series. The producer didn't want this, so I sent this letter.

Dear ...
Let's try it this way. I'll list a number of possible premises, locations, and characters that are flexible enough to allow for the disguise idea. I'll also leave open the question of whether we know or do not know who the killer is early in the story. In other words, the following premises can be whodunits or not as we choose. All of the following are

thrillers with a detection element. I've incorporated your idea of a broader scale and a film approach rather than a television pilot.

#1 MURDER IN DISGUISE
Background
The background in The List of Adrian Messenger was British upper class with the ongoing metaphor of the fox hunt. It is possible to transpose the tale to the American upper class and an appropriate metaphor. The advantage of a running metaphor is that it adds to audience appreciation of game playing.
Premise
Arenas with an upper-class setting that we might consider:
■Gambling—A group of wealthy Americans, old friends, all marked for murder, jet to a Caribbean island to gamble. The odds for survival go down as each is murdered. The central figure, outside of the killer, might well be one of the gamblers, a member of the group who is not on the junket merely for fun but because he/she is (a) trying to trap the killer, (b) nearly broke and in need of money. The climax might well be in a vast casino, empty except for the survivors, who are involved in a high-stakes game of life and death. The game may be interrupted by the revelation of the killer. The central figure can become involved with a member of the jet set group.
■Hunting—A weekend of hunting on a secluded island estate off the coast of Maine soon becomes a murder scene. The central figure might well be a witty but slightly alcoholic character (like Lew Ayres in Holiday, perhaps, or Gig Young in Teacher's Pet) who pulls things together to save a young woman in the group who at first ignores him. Note: Your idea of a big game hunting background in an exclusive resort might well fit this premise.
■Carnival—A real or mythical South American or Caribbean carnival would offer the metaphor of disguise, costume, pretense. It would also be fun to create a mythical carnival complete with rituals that figure into the climax or the solution of the crime.
■Archaeology—An illegal dig in an Arab country would

offer metaphor and running threat of discovery by the country in which the dig is taking place. The dig itself could be undertaken as an expensive amusement by most of the wealthy members of the group but soon become a context for murder with the climax (a) in a museum or (b) at the site of the dig.

■Antiques—A background of antique collection and competition offers the context of wealth and the possibility of a climax at an auction. A McGuffin—priceless jewel box, tiara of Queen Christina, whatever—could be added as a goal of the killer. A final auction at which the killer appears in disguise in the audience would make a perfect climax. How about a chase through the antique warehouse?

Plot

The story would not unfold in this order, but this is a general working plot possibility that would vary with each context.

A member of the original group who committed a murder is thought to be dead by the others, but he is very much alive and decides that he must kill his former acquaintances because he is now quite successful in another field and about to become a very public figure whose face will be on 60 Minutes or the cover of Time. It must be revealed at some point that he is a master of disguise, having specialized in creating his own unique makeup for a variety of roles as an amateur or professional actor.

Jerry, a highly eccentric fringe member of the wealthy group, is hard on the trail of the killer but keeping the information to himself until he has evidence. He shares his suspicions, to some extent, with a member of the group who is most sympathetic, Alex Welles, wealthy, witty, unreliable. Jerry also indicates that he is trying to protect the next victim.

When Jerry is killed, apparently in an accident, he leaves a cryptic message with Ann, the daughter of a member of the group. In spite of the message that Ann tries to give to the police, the police dismiss her suspicions and she turns to Alex.

This situation creates a pair of protagonists who are not

professional detectives but potential victims. It also provides an exotic atmosphere in which to present the tale.
There are a number of possible variations within this general arena. The young woman might well be a working
nurse, model, actress, lawyer, secretary who gets involved
with the wealthy young man she despises but who turns
out to be very helpful and sympathetic. Or, the reverse
could exist. The woman could be the wealthy one and the
young man an unsuccessful lawyer, actor, etc., who happens to be present when Jerry is killed. The coincidence of
his presence at the scene of the murder can turn out to be
no coincidence at all.

#2 THE GAME OF MURDER
Background
Mystery weekends have become very popular.
I've attended/participated in several of these, one at a
rambling, old semi-run-down resort that had once been the
place to go in the Midwest for a luxurious weekend. During
the mystery weekend, a quintet of mystery writers and a
psychic researcher gave talks about their work and partici-
pated in a mock murder mystery with attendees working in
teams to solve the crime and win prizes. The windblown
tennis court, isolated swimming pool, ancient bowling alley
were all scenes where clues could be found. Attendees included businessmen dragged to the place by their wives,
nearly fawning fans of the writers, groups of women who
came with the vague hope of meeting men. The writers
included an alcoholic on the way down, a mystery-writing
judge, a wealthy older male writer with a heart condition,
and a professor who wrote comic mysteries (me). The weekend was organized by a trio of women, one of whom was a
mystery reviewer.
I've also attended a much more elegant mystery weekend
at the Grand Hotel on Mackinac Island. That one had a
1920s motif that included costumes for the writer partici-
pants/actors and attendees. The Mackinac Island weekend
was organized by a husband and wife team who also wrote
the mystery.

Premise

A husband and wife team, perhaps the owners of a small
travel agency, organize the weekend and, much to their
surprise, find the event a great success. On the first night of
the weekend after everyone has arrived by boat (or by car
through the woods if the resort idea is used), the husband
and wife, Michael and Jan, greet the writers and work out
the basic characters and plot of the mystery the attendees
will have to solve. They assign roles, give information, and
indicate that the writers will be suspects to be interviewed
by the various teams at appointed hours after a series of
mock crimes. The participants do not know which of them
is the fictitious killer, though the killer himself (or herself)
knows.

Interesting variation: One of the writers is hired to write
the murder mystery and leave the clues. He/she does not
tell Michael and Jan who the killer is. He/she may even be
working from a basic plot thought up by Michael and Jan.
In any case, the plot of the fictitious tale should be based on
a real case. The writer is both the first victim in the staged
murder mystery and the first real victim of the killer at the
mystery weekend. The writer dies at the opening night
cocktail party while the band plays and vacationers disguised as Inspector Clouseau, Sherlock Holmes, Charlie Chan,
Hercule Poirot, etc., assume the murder is staged.

For a very good combination of reasons, the people on the
island or at the resort become isolated—a terrible storm
combined with the unwillingness of the nearest small-town
police to take them seriously. Perhaps the police think the
murder report is a publicity stunt. More likely, telephone
communication to the outside has been cut off by a storm
or the killer.

In any case, Jan and Michael find that they must solve
the mystery as more victims begin to appear in odd places,
odd because they coincide with the script the dead author
had written. The game goes on for the attendees, who do
not know a real murder has taken place, but for Jan and
Michael it is no game.

Opportunities for disguise are evident—waiters, vacationers, musicians, custodians. The killer's motive might simply

be that he/she believes that the writer set up the situation to catch him/her for the original crime on which the weekend tale was based.

Gradually it becomes clear that the victims of the fictional crime and the ones who are now dying are linked. It also becomes evident that Jan, who plays the third victim, is on the killer's list.

A trap is set for the killer, a ballroom scene in which the attendees, working in teams, give their solutions to the supposedly fictional murders. Michael and Jan indicate that they will announce the dead author's solution (which they do not have). The disguised killer reveals himself/herself and dies horribly on the ballroom stage.

#3 A HEALTHY WAY TO DIE
Background

Health spas, fat farms, and natural retreats for the rich are fertile ground for a thriller. Equipment, pools, steam rooms designed to take off pounds can become quite sinister. The equipment for health can become the tools for death. Opportunities for disguise include overweight clients, visiting diet experts, health food cooks, caretakers, staff members.

Premise

La Pura Health Center is a highly successful spa built around a natural spring on a mountaintop. La Pura is run by Jan and Michael Canfield for the absentee owners. The staff consists of well-built men and women who serve as examples to those who spend a week or two of luxurious misery at the center. La Pura caters to wealthy, overweight women and out-of-shape executives, the worst of whom bribe staff members to smuggle in food or cigars or sneak off to the nearby small town of Calgo during the night for Mexican food.

One evening a flood in the valley below the center knocks out the phone lines and isolates La Pura from the world. The first murder occurs in the exercise room. The victim is a staff member. An eccentric, wealthy woman who claims to know the murderer is the second victim, but she dies in Jan's arms after giving a cryptic dying statement.

Gradually, Michael and Jan realize that the killer is after Jan. A trap is set during an exercise class at which the killer is revealed.

#4 A QUIET NIGHT AT SEA

Background

A luxury cruise in the Caribbean complete with shipboard gambling, semi-celebrity entertainers, swimming pools, and on-deck volleyball and tennis is a likely setting for a terrorist attack. In fact, it has been done. But what if someone wanted to commit murder and blame it on terrorists? Or, perhaps, what if a terrorist assassin went on such a cruise expressly to kill someone, possibly a key industrial or governmental figure, on the cruise?

Premise

Michael Washington's orchestra plays in the lounge of the cruise ship Paloma. Laughter ripples in the evening air, and strollers move around the deck. A lone figure whose face is not seen stalks an older couple. The figure steps forward, strikes in view of at least half a dozen people, and flees into the darkness.

One of the witnesses is the entertainment coordinator, a young woman named Jan. Her powers of observation are a bit better than those of the other witnesses, and she shares her suspicions with her husband, Michael, the orchestra leader.

Several more murders take place—in the ballroom at night, in the ship's galley, in the storeroom. Each murder is described differently by witnesses. Michael and Jan come close to figuring out who the killer might be, but they confide in the wrong person and become potential victims. The killer is unmasked at the shipboard costume ball.

Note: The tale could be set at sea but on a smaller though even more luxurious scale, perhaps a yacht on the way to Greece.

AND SEVERAL OTHER POSSIBLE DIRECTIONS:
#5 A CONVENTIONAL WAY TO DIE

A convention offers possibilities for disguise and game playing.

The convention can be pastime oriented—science fiction, mystery, UFOs, musicologists, opera buffs, fans of old radio or television. A science fiction or television convention would offer the possibility of the chaos of conventions (as in Robert Altman's <u>Health</u>) and disguise (people dressed as Klingons or aliens from <u>V</u> or characters from <u>Buck Rogers, Battle Star Galactica, Space 1999,</u> etc.). It also offers the possibility of an unmasking in a big scene.

#6 MURDER AT THE OPERA
Costume, disguise, massive dark sets, and lonely corridors and subbasements may be reminiscent of the Phantom, but they are also echoes of the Murder at the Met case several years ago in which a female musician was attacked and murdered by a young Metropolitan Opera work crew member. The potential victim can be a young singer who teams up with a member of the troupe to catch the killer. The climax can come high above the opera amid the whirling air-conditioning units and the dark shafts that surround them.

The preceding is a bit condensed and is the second proposal on the basic concept. A third proposal with six more possible areas, various plot variations, and a list of ten characters and their functions followed. A fourth proposal concentrated on the specific context we agreed upon, *Murder in Disguise,* which would take place during a mystery weekend on a small Caribbean island.

The proposal was refined, condensed, and finally pitched to CBS and ABC. ABC showed no interest. CBS showed distinct interest, but nothing has come of it, which is precisely what I expected. If you have one out of ten projects picked up at least to the point of being piloted or even funded for script development, you are doing reasonably well.

Proposals for half-hour comedies are a bit more difficult. An oddity of the industry is that there are hundreds of half-hour comedy pilots—many of them quite good, most of them awful—

that have been shot and never aired. The cost of producing a half-hour studio comedy is high but relatively low compared to the one-hour filmed dramatic show. The irony is that the two-hour movie pilot stands a far greater chance of recouping its cost than the much less expensive comedy.

In your proposal package, the treatment should be a simple, straightforward telling of the episode, scene by scene. Include some dialogue if you wish, but essentially tell the story, making clear who the characters will be and where the action will take place.

Keep it brief. Don't repeat yourself and, remember, don't include anything in your treatment that doesn't transpose into action and dialogue. Minimize description and stay away from describing the feelings or thoughts of the characters. Write your treatment so that the reader can imagine the tale unfolding before him as if it were a television episode.

All right. You've written your proposal. What do you do with it? The same thing you do with everything else you write: get a producer to look at it or find an agent. Again, we will cover these topics in Chapter Eleven.

Remember, the chances are quite slim that a proposal will get a beginner into the industry, but the ones who succeed are the ones who try in spite of the odds. It helps if you have talent. It helps if you know what you are doing. It helps if you know someone or if you get lucky. Getting to know somebody and getting lucky can be worked at.

Case in point: I wrote dozens of short stories, several plays, and five novels by the time I was thirty-five. I sold none of the novels, had five of the short stories published (total income from short stories: $380), and had one short play published and produced (no income at all here, only six copies of the published play and an invitation to see the play produced in New York. I couldn't go. I couldn't afford the train fare). I kept writing. I knew I would keep writing even if no one ever produced a film of mine or published a novel. I might get bitter. I might become resentful, but I had enough faith in my talent and enough desire to write that I wouldn't and couldn't stop.

In the past ten years, I have had twenty-three books published (one of which was recently filmed), have written three feature films that have been produced, have had half a dozen short stories published, have worked on five television series, and am working on the script for a made-for-television film and on a theatrical film for MGM as I write this book. I had no connections when I started, hadn't the slightest idea of how to get an agent, and had never seen a script.

How was I able to accomplish this? I sent my work to agents and kept writing.

CHAPTER
5

CREATING CHARACTERS

Occasionally a script will sell because its story is so unusual and so "good" that it can't be ignored. More often, far more often, it will sell because the characters are so vivid and the dialogue so sharp that the producer or actor who reads it can easily imagine it coming to life. Unfortunately, novice writers usually seem to have trouble creating characters.

Harlan Ellison:

"For characterization, beginners limit it to 'He's just like Gary Cooper, only his ears are bigger.' "

When you are writing a spec script, the characters already exist. Your task is to learn about the characters, watch them, listen to them carefully, absorb them, imagine them in scenes, imagine them reading the dialogue you create.

Casting in Your Imagination

When you are writing a miniseries or a made-for-television adaptation of a novel, the characters already exist, but they have no visual persona. They exist only in your imagination. You must bring them to life through that imagination. I suggest a first step in adapting for television is to cast the role in your imagination, to imagine actors who would play those roles and to imagine them saying the lines you create. It doesn't matter whether the actors you imagine are the ones who actually get the parts. If the character is clear and vivid and the dialogue good, a capable actor will make it his or her own.

The same is true of original scripts you write. I suggest you cast them not with your friends and relatives but with actors. The reason for not using your friends is that you tend to lock the character into the personality of a real person, a person with a history known to you that you can't alter. Even if a character you create is based on a friend or an enemy, do your imaginary casting with an actor.

Seldom have I written with the actor or actress who actually played the part in mind. For example, when I was hired by Sergio Leone to cowrite the screenplay for *Once Upon a Time in America*, I was told to imagine Paul Newman, George C. Scott, and Tom Berenger in principal roles. My dialogue writing and development of characters proceeded from this assumption, and it made the job much easier. When Robert DeNiro was signed to play one of the principal roles, I worked with him to revise character and dialogue, but the changes were not massive. The adjustments were in the details, the reconsideration of character. I knew from the start when writing *A Woman in the Wind*, a television special, that the producer/writer wanted Colleen Dewhurst for the lead. I wrote with Ms. Dewhurst in mind, imagined her voice, listened to and watched her in movies and on television. She read the script and accepted the role. For the second lead in the film, a male, I cast Raul Julia in my imagination. I could imagine him delivering the monologues, casting a spell on the woman played by Dewhurst. I didn't simply write. I imagined. I listened. I recorded and anticipated seeing the results, seeing if the finished film matched my imagination. As it turned out, Julia did not do the part. Jay O. Sanders, who is tall and blond, played the role I had imagined for Julia, who is dark and slight. Their voices are different. Their bearing is different. Adjustments again had to be made, but the basic character was there for Sanders to see. It didn't have to be re-created.

As a final example, when I wrote the film *Enemy Territory,* my imaginary cast consisted of Brian Dennehy, Howard Rollins, Jr., and Moses Gunn. When the film was made, it starred Gary Frank, Ray Parker, Jr., and Jan-Michael Vincent. Again, the script and characters were vivid to the actors and the director, and only minor changes had to be made. Gary Frank is younger, smaller, more vulnerable than Dennehy. The character, as interpreted by Frank, is less aggressive, more frightened. Ray Parker, Jr., whose only major acting before the film had been in music videos, particularly *Ghostbusters* and an episode of *Gimme a Break,* came remarkably close to my vision of the character, though Parker played him more heroically and with less vulnerability than I had imagined. The most extreme change came with Jan-Michael Vincent being cast in the role I had imagined for Moses Gunn. Gunn is a black actor in his sixties. Vincent is white and in his thirties. Remarkably, only a few words had to be changed. The character, a crazed veteran, came across quite vividly.

The important thing is that the character was tangible to me. All the characters were part of me, hints of others.

Creating a New Character

How do you create these characters?

Part of the creation of character seems magical, but it isn't. Once you have an idea for a character, have the broad outline of that character, and have cast the character in your imagination either with actors currently playing those roles or actors you imagine in the original script or adaptation you are preparing, you begin playing a game. Let the character move, think, act scenes. Don't write the scenes. Imagine them. Let the character come to life.

While standing in line at the supermarket, a feisty old woman pushes in front of you in line. What would your main character do? What would your other characters do? How would your character react to a madwoman who stops your character and insists that the world will end at midnight that day, to being held up by an armed teenager, to being told by a doctor that he or she needs serious surgery, to finding an abandoned infant, to losing a shoe in the middle of a bustling downtown area?

Create your own situations or remember those that have faced you and imagine the difference between your own reaction and that of your character.

General rule: Tragedy is based on the assumption that the characters are somehow superior to you and the assumed reader/reviewer. Romances/thrillers are based on the assumption that the characters are equal to the reader/viewer. Comedy is based on the assumption that the reader/viewer is superior to the character(s).

This general rule applies not only to the broad genres and characters within them indicated here. For example, the classical detective story—the Sherlock Holmes, Hercule Poirot, Jessica Fletcher tale—is based on the tragic assumption that the central character is superior to those of us reading/viewing. The classical detective knows things we do not know, withholds information from us. We are, as far as information is concerned, at the mercy of the great detective. Frequently in such tales a comic character, a character below us, exists to observe and comment on the tale. The viewer/reader is placed between the superior and inferior figures. The difficulty in writing both tragedy and comedy is one of imagining characters much different from ourselves.

The ability of the writer to imagine, to empathize, is most important, therefore, in tragedy and comedy, and easier in romance, ''naturalistic'' tales.

In creating characters it is absolutely essential, therefore, that at the first-draft level you let the characters take over, letting them carry on complete conversations and actions in your imagination. When I begin a comedy script, I normally have one or two jokes or funny reactions in mind. Sometimes I don't even have that. I simply have a story, situations. I create characters to whom the viewer and I will be superior. I create them, empathize with them, and put them into situations. Then I imagine them working their way out of or into problems, imagine them reacting. The humor comes from the character. If the character is full, well realized, tangible, the humor will come from him or her, depending on the situations you have created.

Observation: If you have to stop and ask yourself ''What would he do next?'' you are in trouble. The trick is to create characters so vivid to you that you don't have to wonder what they will do. You observe them doing it and you record it. That doesn't mean you won't go back and sharpen dialogue, remove dead ends, make changes to better suggest the direction you finally take. But you'll usually find, in both comedy and tragedy at the extremes, that your best writing, your best development and presentation of character, will be in a spontaneous first draft *if your characters are well realized and vivid*.

People watch television for characters and story. Actually the two are inseparable, but if one has to be given more credit, it is character, particularly in series television. People turn on their favorite shows or choose new ones because of the characters, the people they want to see and hear each week.

Finding Sources for Characters

Where do these characters come from?

Again, all of them are, must be, part of you. You must be able to project, empathize. If you are unable to truly empathize, to let the character take over, you'll find, as so many writers have, that everyone in your script talks alike, thinks alike, is alike. And you will have a dull script.

You find characters by imagining, projecting, wondering. I create major characters because I'm curious about how they will behave, what they will think.

Examples: I write a series of detective novels, the Toby Peters series. My central character, Toby Peters, who is obviously me and not me, was created when I wondered what Philip Marlowe would have been like if he had a low self-image and Harry Orwell's bad back. I cast the character in my imagination (character actor Richard Bakalayan) and began to create a biography for Toby *before* I wrote a single word of the first book. I didn't write out the biography, but writing it out is a good idea, and eventually, after five books, I did write the biography.

I surrounded Toby with supporting characters, series regulars, including:

■ Sheldon Minck—a myopic, rotund, bald dentist in his fifties who smokes soggy cigars and is less than antiseptic. Sheldon was suggested by a dentist I went to as a child who worked on patients while he smoked and talked constantly about his problems. I cast Sheldon (Sorrell Booke).

■ Jeremy Butler—The landlord of Toby's office building. An ex-wrestler who is now a landlord and poet. Jeremy is a hulking bald man who is slow to anger and quite philosophical. Jeremy is based on a character in Stanley Kubrick's film *The Killing,* a philosophical chess-playing wrestler played by a real wrestler (Kola Kwariani). I always imagine the actor when I think of Jeremy. I liked the character Kubrick created so much that I wanted to keep him alive and did so in Jeremy. The wrestler in Kubrick's film speaks with a heavy European accent that is very difficult to decipher. I made Jeremy very precise and articulate.

In one of my books, I cast my future wife as the central figure and imagined how she would react to a variety of rather terrifying situations. The book, *When the Dark Man Calls,* has been filmed with Catherine Deneuve, who looks nothing like my wife, in the role.

The hero of another series of books I wrote is a Russian police inspector named Porfiry Petrovich Rostnikov. I first read Dostoyevsky's *Crime and Punishment* when I was about twelve and was more fascinated by the detective, Porfiry Petrovich, than by the tragic central character, Roskolnikov. I thought Porfiry Petrovich deserved his own story. I wanted to read, see that story. In a sense, my Porfiry Petrovich Rostnikov is the descendant of the original. I cast the French actor Philippe Noiret in my imagination as my Rostnikov.

The important point is that I created these characters because I was interested in and fascinated by them. I wanted to see more of them. I created them because I wanted to enjoy the experience—identify with—them.

Creating Character Biographies

One way to establish biographies for your characters is to do what I did in the Toby Peters example. Create the character before you write and imagine that biography. Another way is to prepare your story and treatment. When you come to a new character in the treatment, write the character's name on a sheet of paper or enter it in your computer. When you finish your treatment, go back to the list of names and prepare biographies for them. If you find it difficult simply to prepare a written biography, use a standard form that you create to fill in information on each character and keep a file on each character. Include information you might never use. The point, once again, is to create a fully developed individual in your imagination.

Here is a form you can use if you don't want to create your own:

CHARACTER:

DATE OF BIRTH: PLACE OF BIRTH:

SIBLINGS (dates of birth, places of birth);

PARENTS (dates of birth, places of birth)

    MOTHER (background, parents, siblings, education, experience):

    FATHER (background, parents, siblings, education, experience):

CHARACTER'S EDUCATION:

CHARACTER'S WORK EXPERIENCE:

CHARACTER'S PRESENT ADDRESS AND OCCUPATION:

CHARACTER'S PRINCIPAL FRIENDS AND ACQUAINTANCES:

CHARACTER'S HOUSE OR APARTMENT (What does it look like?):

CHARACTER'S WORK ENVIRONMENT, IF ANY (What does it look like?):

PHYSICAL DESCRIPTION OF CHARACTER (including height and weight):

WHAT KIND OF CAR DOES CHARACTER OWN, IF ANY?

WHAT CLOTHES DOES HE OR SHE HAVE IN THE CLOSET?

NAME AND LOCATION OF THE CHARACTER'S PHYSICIAN, DENTIST, LAWYER:

DOES CHARACTER HAVE ANY ONGOING MEDICAL PROBLEMS?

WHEN WAS THE LAST TIME CHARACTER WENT TO A PHYSICIAN AND FOR WHAT?

WHERE DOES CHARACTER SHOP FOR GROCERIES, IF APPLICABLE?

The point of the form should be fairly evident. The idea is to get you thinking about your characters, to make them more

clear and concrete to you when you write them, to get you to
know the character, to see the character.

EXERCISE 6

—You might want to incorporate some of these questions in your written
biography. Answer these questions as quickly as you can. The more vivid the
character is to you, the easier it will be to answer the questions. Answering will
also give the character life. Think of your own questions beyond these.

- What is your character's favorite food? What food does the
  character hate?
- What is your character's favorite relative, color, place to visit,
  sport, game, item of clothing, author, film, television show or
  series, actor?
- What did your character enjoy in school? What did he or she
  hate?
- How much money does your character have? Where is the
  money?
- Does your character have a best friend or friends? Who are
  they? Describe your character's voice.
- Cast your character: What actor would play him or her?
- Does your character sleep well? If the character has dreams,
  what kind of dreams are they?
- Where does your character get the laundry done?
- Does your character currently have a pet? Did your character
  ever have a pet? What kind of pet and what happened to it?
- Is there some characteristic of your character that he or she
  recognizes and either likes or dislikes?

You get the idea. Obviously, some of the questions won't be
relevant to some characters, but most will.

EXERCISE 7

—One way to explore and expand your ability to develop characters is to endow the character with a particular perspective and tell the story from that perspective. This not only gives you an exercise in perspective, it can also make you deal with perspectives and points of view you might ordinarily avoid. You may find that you can do much more than you give yourself credit for being able to do. So, take the story that follows and write a one-page monologue from as many of the points of view as you can. It's best if you can do them all. Write the story as:

(a) a deaf old woman;
(b) a person with an acute sense of smell;
(c) a highly religious man;
(d) a blind person;
(e) a six-year-old;
 (f) a beautiful teen-age girl;
(g) a handsome male lifeguard;
(h) a police officer;
 (i) a rock musician;
 (j) a shy woman with an acute sense of color.

The story, which is purposely without major incident so that you will concentrate on character, goes as follows: A man and woman come out of an ice cream store. They are observed by the person who will tell the story. The man and woman argue about whether to go home or go out for dinner. They go down the street arguing and fail to see a woman carrying grocery bundles. They bump into the woman, whose bundles fall. The arguing man and woman help the woman pick up her bundles and then go on their way, continuing their argument. Our interested narrator, perhaps going in the same direction by chance, follows. The arguing couple stops in a park near a fountain. They make up and agree to go out for dinner. Just as they make up, they spot the narrator and approach him or her, indicating that they are upset because they have been followed.

Explore and expand the aspects of character and the kinds of character that might not be completely familiar to you. Too often neglected in developing character are the senses of touch and smell. Sounds are often overlooked. You can often intrigue an actor by giving him or her something to develop that is peculiar to that character. Perhaps the character likes to touch cool objects or get physically too close to others during conversations. Or conversely, perhaps the character doesn't like people to come too close. It doesn't have to be obsessional behavior, perhaps not even something other characters or an audience would consciously notice, but it can give a hint, direction to the actor and director about how to play the character. However, simply giving the character a trait that doesn't relate to the character's personality or problems is distracting rather than a contribution. So, if you have a person who guards his emotions, who won't let other people know how he feels, it might be reasonable to suggest that the character wouldn't want to be physically close to others. Conversely, a character who desires friends because he has had none might want to get very close, perhaps too close for others.

There are only two ways audiences can get to know your characters, by what the characters say and by what they do. The next chapter discusses the former; this chapter has discussed the latter. Remember, character is action, not just dialogue.

6

WRITING DIALOGUE

You can be a highly successful writer if you can't think of a single story, but you can't be a successful writer if you can't create charters or write dialogue.

Harlan Ellison on Producers and Production Executives:

''When they 'read' scripts, they don't read the whole script. What they read is dialogue. They don't read the stage directions, so they don't realize when they complain that a certain character is superfluous in a scene because he never says a word . . . that he exited in the preceding shot!''

Bill Nuss on One of the Biggest Problems in Spec Scripts Submitted by Beginners:

''Redundancy of dialogue. People saying 'Something I gotta tell you.' 'What?' 'Well, maybe I shouldn't tell you.' 'Oh, come on, what is it?' 'It's kinda important.' 'It's important?' 'Yeah.' ''

Garry Marshall on the same subject:

"One, they make all the characters talk the same. There's no delineation or differentiation (big words with a *d*) between characters, so they can be played by anybody. Two, in a running series, they do not capture the character created by the creators of the series."

Dialogue and character are, in the final analysis, inseparable, but there are ways of concentrating on and improving your ability to write dialogue.

This chapter will, if you do the exercises, take longer than the previous chapters, but the effort will be worth the time. Once again, reading it is not enough. You have to do it.

So, here is the first thing to do.

EXERCISE 8

—Write the scene described below. Write it in simple form; simply indicate who the speaker is and include a minimum of description. Allow yourself no more than half an hour, even if you are not finished, and do not read the information on the scene until you are ready to start. As soon as you read the information, begin the exercise. Don't stop to think about it. Just do it. Try to make the scene complete and coherent, with a beginning, a middle, and an end. Use only the characters given to write your scene.

The scene: A couple walks down a stairway talking, absorbed in their plans for the day. Before they reach the bottom of the stairs one of the two trips on a bird and tumbles down the remaining stairs. Lee rushes in, sees the injured bird, and begins to scream.

That's it. Write the scene to that point and then go on to a conclusion. Do it, as I said, in half an hour and start now. Don't read further until you do so.

Okay. Now that you've finished, ask yourself some questions about what you've done before we get to the central issue of dialogue.

1. What kind of couple did you create? Most people, given the assignment, will assume that we are talking about a married

couple or a couple living together. There are other couples: a couple of kids, a couple going out on a blind date, an old man and his granddaughter or daughter, an old woman and her grandson or son, a gay couple. The choice was yours.

2. Is Lee a man or a woman? Young or old? It makes a difference, doesn't it?

3. Did you cast the characters in your imagination? Whom did you cast and why?

4. Are you pleased with what you have done? Most of the people in my classes over the years have been reasonably pleased with their work on this exercise; which points out that writing quickly does not necessarily mean writing badly. In fact, some people write much better when they do it quickly, when they must give power to their imagination rather than their intellect.

5. What kind of bird got hurt? A parakeet? An ostrich? A parrot? Was it even a live bird? It could have been stuffed. I've had students add an extra "character" to the scene by having the bird be a talking parrot.

6. How badly hurt is the person who fell down the stairs? Your decision could determine whether the scene is comedy or tragedy.

In writing your scene, did you make use of anything you've read in the book up to this point? Remember, this book works only if you use it, so make the suggestions part of your tools.

Now let's tackle the issue of dialogue.

What do you want when you write dialogue? What do you want the viewer/listener to hear?

Normally, you want to create the illusion of reality, the illusion of natural discourse. Of course there are genres in which you might want a heightened or alternate way of speaking— some comedy, perhaps science fiction or fantasy, or perhaps certain historical tales. But generally, even if you are writing comedy, science fiction, or historical drama, you want to give the audience the illusion that they are listening to real people talk. How do you do that? Did you do that in the exercise? Would a producer or an agent pick up your script and easily be able to imagine human beings delivering the lines?

Put your scene aside for the moment and do the next exercise.

EXERCISE 9

—Find a small tape recorder. If you don't own one, you should buy one if you can afford it. If you have to borrow or rent one, do so. Take the tape recorder someplace where you can secretly record a conversation, preferably among three people. It's best if you are not one of the three. The easiest time and place to do this is during a meal or at a meeting. Record about five minutes and try to get the start of the conversation. When you have the conversation recorded, transcribe it on paper. Write it out using the same format you used in Exercise 8 and do it as faithfully as possible. Indicate pauses by using ellipses (. . .) and use parentheses ( ) for passages you simply can't hear well enough to transcribe.
When you've finished the exercise, read on.

A comparison of Exercise 8 and Exercise 9 will probably reveal something rather disconcerting—*the tape recorder writes better dialogue than you do.*

By "better" I mean that it reads and sounds more authentic than your dialogue because it contains the specifics of human speech.

The task now is to identify the specifics of human speech and to start incorporating them into your scripts. This doesn't mean that you should let the style of "realism" take over and distract from the balance of story, character, and dialogue. It means that you should have the means of natural dialogue available to you to use and control.

You've heard people speaking all your life. Now you have to start listening to the way they speak—their patterns, quirks, nuances. You have to become a close listener. Carry a notebook and eavesdrop. Delight in the odd but real phrase or pattern and use it.

These are some of the things you may note in your transcription of the secretly recorded conversation:

■ People sometimes do not finish their thoughts or sentences.

■ People sometimes fail to finish a thought or a sentence and then come back and finish that thought or sentence after they have interjected another, possibly related, idea.

■ People frequently do not listen to each other and do not respond directly to what the other person has said because they have something they want to say, something more important to them than what the other person is saying.

■ People repeat the same sentence, the same idea, sometimes the same word.

■ Even educated people do not always speak grammatically.

■ People sometimes speak in single words or phrases rather than complete sentences.

Examples of these characteristics of speech can be seen in this short passage of dialogue:

TODD
I can't stand it anymore, can't stand it anymore, Angie. You know what I mean? Sometimes ... I tell you he drives me nuts ... I want to just scream at him. If he ever ...

ANGIE
My father and mother are like that. Awful. Always at each other. My father and mother are just like that.

■ People may use certain phrases characteristic of them, which they repeat as punctuation and emphasis. Examples: "You understand . . ." "Don't you know?" "You see?" "Eh?" "As a matter of fact . . ."

■ Descriptive sounds—sounds that might not easily be tran-

scribed but that help to establish the illusion of reality—may be used more or less by different individuals.
Example:

TODD
So, I hit him with the broom, right with the broom, whuuumph, as hard as I can, and he goes flying across the room like he was launched or something, know what I mean?

■ Some people speak more precisely and carefully when they are angry or under stress. Others lose control of language and expression.

The list can go on and, in fact, you should make such a list, but more importantly, you should start to listen consciously to the way other people speak, even the way you speak. You can learn a lot from listening to yourself, as strange as that may seem.

It's important to stress that the illusion of reality in dialogue is just that, an illusion, something for you to use and utilize. If a character fails to complete a thought or a sentence, it may be that he is unwilling to face what he was going to say. A character may repeat a phrase like "you understand?" because she feels misunderstood at a deeper level than conversation. If a character repeats a word or a sentence, perhaps that word or sentence is even more important to him than it appears to be on the surface. The choice is yours.

PART
TWO

GENRES AND FORMS

The next four chapters detail four of the most important genres and forms of television writing:

■ The police tale: an enduringly popular genre on television since television began.

■ Television comedy: another genre that has been around as long as television has and continues to be an extremely popular form today.

We examine these genres in detail, delineating their conventions and stressing how a beginning writer can learn and use these conventions to produce professional scripts.

■ Made-for-television movies and miniseries: these important forms allow the beginning writer to come up with, respectively, original ideas (as opposed to spec scripts) and adaptations. Therefore, these forms represent a departure from the police tale and narrative comedy genres.

■ Television documentary: this nonfiction form offers another market for the beginning writer. We discuss both the mainstream and the vérité documentary in the last chapter of Part Two.

The chapters on both the made-for-television movie and the documentary discuss in detail the components and the conventions of those forms along with tips on generating salable ideas and developing them to script length.

CHAPTER
7

WRITING THE POLICE TALE

Before you begin writing for a specific series or genre, it is a good idea to study and understand that genre and its conventions.

Within the broad category of crime and detection can be found a significant percentage, possibly a majority, of one-hour television series and made-for-television films. Each subcategory or kind has its own conventions that the writer should understand. The conventions for the private detective series—*Magnum, P.I., Simon and Simon, Mike Hammer, Moonlighting,* and *Spenser: For Hire*—are quite different from series that deal specifically with the police—*Hunter, Miami Vice, Cagney & Lacey, Crime Story, Sledge Hammer, Hill Street Blues.*

Let's look at the differences between the so-called mystery and thriller genres with an eye to defining what is expected or required in writing a story or series that concentrates on the police or individual police officers. We could concentrate on a variety of series or episodic genres, including the private detective, the melodrama and science fiction, but purely as examples we will concentrate first on the police tale to provide a model for studying other genres and then on the half-hour comedy, which is an ongoing and major market for writers.

Origins of the Police Tale

As I indicated above, police tales are often categorized together with tales about private detectives, criminals, and spies. Television series about criminals are generally not practical, though made-for-television films centering on the criminal are quite common. The reason is simple. The series requires that the central figure or figures reappear in each episode. Sustaining the criminal character without having him or her brought to justice is highly problematic, but, it has been done, as in *The Gangster Chronicles* and *The Untouchables* (which featured Al Capone and Frank Nitti as continuing characters).

Unlike other popular forms such as the western, the melodrama, or the horror story, police tales have a relatively brief history, with roots in the nineteenth century. For the most part the police did not exist as a separate profession until the nineteenth century. Those who apprehended criminals before this time were soldiers, as they still are in Italy and some other countries, or extensions of the judicial system, as in contemporary Soviet Russia. In England, a police force was established when the judges started to pay people—usually "reformed" criminals—out of their own budgets to go out and catch criminals.

Novels and stories about the police officer came slightly after the rise of the police force in nineteenth-century Europe. In France, such stories predated this slightly, because the police force was established as a separate entity from the army after the French Revolution. A transitional tale, Victor Hugo's *Les Misérables* (a public domain story that was the inspiration for one of the most successful series in television history, *The*

Fugitive), began the pattern. Initially police tales—and many existed in the previous century—were presented as true-crime reports and not as fiction, in spite of the latitude authors often gave themselves. Alan Pinkerton, who founded the Pinkerton Detective Agency, which still exists, promoted his own exploits as true police tales in books and periodicals with great success.

Almost from the inception of storytelling in the medium, police tales became a staple of television. *Dragnet* may have been one of the first, but it was far from the only example (*Racket Squad, M Squad, Highway Patrol,* and *Rocky King* are all early examples) of the genre in its half-hour format. Today's television police tales are all one hour long. The most recent half-hour police tale was *Sledge Hammer,* which might more reasonably be categorized as a comedy/police tale.

Critical attention to these and current police tales on television has tended to focus on whether or not the series or particular episodes are accurate in their depiction of police work and whether they are too violent.

The problem for the writer who gets caught up in the realist argument is that while viewers do want the illusion of reality, the same illusion we try to capture in dialogue, they probably do not want the actuality of police procedure and routine as regular weekly fare. A friend and I conceived a pilot for the most realistic police tale ever done. We were sure it would fail, and it did. The treatment for the first episode read as follows.

Real Police
Patrolman Watkins and Patrolwoman Ennis are in their car on a hot summer day. They cruise the streets of the city, listening to calls on their radio and looking out for suspicious characters or incidents. Generally, they talk about their families, financial problems, where they are going to take their coffee break and have lunch. They get two calls: a domestic disturbance that proves to be a false alarm and a possible breaking and entering that proves to be a window

accidentally broken by kids playing baseball. They stop one driver, an old woman, for having a dragging muffler, and they are called upon to direct traffic at a busy intersection where the traffic light goes out. On the way in from their shift they see a suspicious-looking man hurrying into an alley. They follow and find that he is dumping a bag of garbage illegally. They decide to warn him instead of giving him a ticket. Back at the station they report that their patrol car needs some minor work.

There are some possibilities for mild comedy here, but when treated as pure realism, normal police work does not translate into exciting adventure. Police stories on television are more about the fantasy life of the audience than the experience of the police.

Several kinds of police tales have been shown on television: those that involve an individual investigator or pair of investigators, such as *Columbo* and *Hunter*; those that involve uniformed officers, such as *T. J. Hooker, Adam 12,* and *CHiPs*: and those that concentrate on an ensemble effort by the police, such as *Hill Street Blues* and *Crime Story*.

Characteristics of Television Police

In plain clothes or uniform, the central character in a television police series has an inevitable commitment to the norm, to the status quo, to keeping things the way they are. Related to this is the convention that the police detective is not usually highly intelligent. He or she may not be a fool, but with rare exceptions intelligence is not a part of television's heroic definition of the police officer. *Columbo,* obviously, was one of those exceptions. *Sledge Hammer* is a comic recognition of this element of the genre.

The virtue and possible defect of the television police detective is his commitment to the rule of law and the protection of the populace, which can often become obsessive. If, for example, the police officer has a family, the police officer's commitment to the job may threaten the family situation. That familial tension is often the basis for the second problem in an episode of a police series.

In some ways the police tale on television has become an urban substitute for the western, which is no longer a popular television form. As in the western, the hero in early police shows was inevitably male. In recent years, police tales have offered female protagonists within what was once an exclusively male community. Potentially interesting series ideas and episodes exploring the differences between television's male and female police remain to be done.

Another characteristic of both uniformed and nonuniform police tales is the importance of partnership. One does not work alone. One is part of a social group. Again, this is quite different from the private forms. Private detectives may have, but usually do not need, partners. On television they traditionally work alone or with helpers who are not equal to them. *Simon and Simon*, obviously, is an exception. The exploration of male/female relationships, a combining of comedy/romance/ private detective genres has been explored in such series as *Remington Steele* and *Moonlighting*. Frequently, people supposedly helping the private detective prove to be more impediment than aid. But the police officer is dependent on other people. There is a primary relationship with a partner or team. The work situation becomes the primary social support for the television police officer. The police officer tends to live within his or her job.

Again, domestic tension becomes the basis for antagonism or even secondary plot. The neglected spouse who says "You spend more time with your partner than you do with me" is familiar in the police genre. It may, in fact, reflect at an exaggerated level the viewer's tension as a worker or spouse in terms of time spent on the job and at home.

Work in the television police tale is a way of living. The partnership is established as one of dependent parts. The police tend to be successful only when they get along and work together. When one is removed or made vulnerable, the others are endangered.

Criminals

The officer's relationship to the police force seems to depend on the nature of the criminal. Much of the criticism of police tales on television has stressed that, with the exception of some uniformed-police tales, the shows do not deal with the real nature of most crime. The criticism is, in one sense, quite true. The overwhelming majority of criminal cases in actuality are domestic, people harming people they know. This, coupled with routine and petty crime, takes up most police time. However, the police tales we see on television are not about real crime and seldom have been. They present, instead, a mythology about crimes that are symbolically important to the viewer.

In television, the overwhelming majority of crimes fall into two categories that may be mythically important but exist only in small numbers in reality. The two kinds of criminals predominantly presented on television are individual lunatics and organized crime figures (Mafia, street gangs, drug gangs, terrorists). Organized crime and individual madness are opposites. Each represents something the police officers (and, obviously, the writer) must handle in a different way. When the television show defines the criminal as insane, the individual police officer assigned to the case tends to grow more and more alienated from his or her partner and other officers. The central detective becomes obsessed with catching the mad killer. Since the detective team represents a unified whole, the existence of the lunatic, who is a fragmented personality, mocks the existence of the team and the social response to the threat he or she poses. The hero, in dealing with a lunatic, comes more and more to see that lunatic as a disease to be wiped out and often as a reflection of the officer's own dark side. The hero is impelled to operate the way the lunatic operates and moves outside the law toward emotionalism and violence.

Unlike film, which moves to a final violent confrontation between lunatic and police officer (*Dirty Harry* and *Lethal Weapon* are prime examples), in television the obsessed police officer tends to pull back at the last minute, to regain his equilibrium and "come to his senses" before the violent confrontation. Alternatively, the hero is freed from responsibility by being forced to destroy the mad villain violently after making it clear that the hero has changed his mind about resolving the situation through violence. One reason for this is simple. The cop has to be back for the next episode. A conscious breaking of the law changes the direction of the series and the image of the police officer. The police officer pulls back or is pulled back and rejoins his or her supportive group before an act that will permanently separate that officer from society is committed. Still, the lunatic is a kind of divisive force, threatening the cooperative effort. That potential, even dominant, use of such characters should be known to you so that you can accept it or play variations on it. Remember, however, that the audience expects both invention and convention, familiarity and variation. Know the conventions, use them, and try to find ways to vary them.

On the other end of the spectrum, when the criminal is a member of organized crime, the police officer tends to work more closely with the members of his or her group. The criminal organization is presented as paralleling the police organization so that there are two institutionalized forces opposing each other. What usually leads to the downfall of organized crime in a police tale is the criminal body's need for direction from above. If the police can get the key figure, the leader, the organization crumbles. This is not necessarily the way gangs or organized crime really works, but, mythically, it functions that way in television episodes because organized crime is presented as a patriarchy (and, rarely, as a matriarchy). We watch the crumbling of one family (criminal, distorted) in the face of another, the police family.

The police, in contrast to organized criminals on television, are well trained and can function without a hierarchy. The criminals are totally dependent on their rules, their parental figures. The police can be hampered by the rules of law, but unlike the criminals, they are not dependent on their hierarchy. There is no single person a criminal can "get" in the police force to stop an investigation.

When the police on television go after "Mr. Big," they are hampered because they have to work within the law. In the confrontation between a police officer and a representative of organized crime, the criminal frequently says "You can't touch me; I know my rights. I'll plead the Fifth Amendment. I want a lawyer." The police, in such situations, are frustrated because the law has prevented them from protecting society. The police on television may stretch the law, but they are ultimately fettered by it. In contrast, organized crime is limited by the fact that, once the key person is eliminated, the entire structure fails.

Both the organized-crime figures and the lunatics are presented as being intellectually or experientially superior to the police. What the police have going for them is a commitment to law and, even more important, a commitment to the populace, to protecting the people. They have the determination to persevere, to protect the people. The police are not tireless, but they are replaceable. It is determination, not intellect, that allows the television cop to overcome the criminal.

Order and Individualism

The police on television tend to have parental figures, superiors within the department, to whom they are drawn for support and advice and whom they frequently reject, in spite of their good advice, because of the individual police officer's obsession. Ultimately, the hero does not need or want to accept the advice of the parental figure, who invariably counsels obeying the law and following orders. This conflict between the hero's commitment to law and order and the hero's need to move outside its limits to protect society relates to a basic motif of the police tale. The moment of anguish that is depicted over and over again in these police tales is that moment in which the hero has to make this decision. In a continuing series the myth demands that whatever the hero decides will be made right. If the officer moves outside the law or ignores orders from a superior, the tale will affirm that decision and find a way to protect him or her from major punishment. On the other hand, if he decides to stay with the law, that decision will be affirmed. No matter what is done, in almost every case the hero's action will be confirmed as correct under the circumstances.

Creating a Lower-Middle-Class Hero

Social class is very important in police tales, as it is in all kinds of crime tales. Classical tales, from the adventures of Sherlock Holmes to those of Jessica Fletcher on *Murder, She Wrote,* are about upper-middle-class or even upper-class heroes.

Such heroes mingle with or are wealthy or professional. Such detectives are called in after the commission of a crime because they are assumed to have special talents and special abilities.

On the other hand, private detectives like Mike Hammer and Spenser are strongly middle-class and slightly outside of society.

Television police, however, fall within a much more limited category of class and background. Cops are lower-middle-class and are committed to protecting the values of that group, which, by the way, comprises the vast majority of television viewers.

In police tales criminals are seeking something from society that the police officer, the people he or she protects, and the viewers watching do not have. Criminals on television want large sums of money or the freedom to act out their wishes and fantasies, which are normally denied the cop and the audience because of the restrictions of law, morality, and convention. Corruption, among both criminals and police, in television cop tales is very specific. Somebody is identified as "bad." We know who it is. He or she gets caught and that ends the evil. In the other genres, private eye tales, for example, or even in our lives, guilt is seldom so clear and specific.

The Structure of the Police Show

While you do have the option of altering the pattern, the narrative pattern of police tales exists for a reason. It is familiar, fulfills the functions I have outlined, and provides the framework for the particular kind of moral tale that characterizes the police show.

The pattern, which provides a model for treatments for a police episode, is as follows.

1. The tale begins with the *commission of a crime*. This

immediately gives us information the police do not have, which places us in a position superior to the hero's.

2. An officer, *the hero, is assigned to the case by chance.* The cop has no personal ties to the case. Obviously, variations can be played in which there is an immediate personal tie, but these are rare. The second problem, usually involving the central figure's partner, is introduced. The problem often reflects the central figure's problem. For example, if Cagney is involved in trying to deal with a criminal who tried to kill her and who she fears will escape punishment in his trial, Lacey may be involved in what proves to be an unfounded fear of a recently released criminal who threatened her years earlier at his trial.

3. *The destruction widens.* The lunatic kills another apparently random victim, or organized criminals blow up one more Vietnamese restaurant. The villain always commits at least two crimes. Whatever the specific nature of the acts, the crimes become more personal to the hero. Perhaps the hero knows the random victim or a relative of the victim, or the random victim bears a painful resemblance to someone the hero knows, or in questioning a relative of the victim the hero begins to identify with the victim. As the crimes continue, they start happening to people who represent something particular and personal to the police officer. In a made-for-television movie or a miniseries and sometimes in an individual one-hour episode, the officer will begin to neglect his or her personal life and relationships.

4. *The quest becomes more and more obsessive,* and the hero behaves less and less rationally.

5. *The hero meets the criminal.* Sometimes this takes place a bit earlier or later, but it is usually in step 5. Sometimes it is a chance meeting. The hero doesn't know the criminal is the one who committed the crime and, possibly, the criminal doesn't know the hero is the person pursuing him or her. Sometimes the police officer does know but does not have the evidence to hold the culprit. But there is some meeting, perhaps a confrontation,

and then the criminal gets away. This usually involves a chase either immediately before the face-to-face confrontation or after it.

6. *The warning.* Someone—spouse, partner, superior—warns the police officer about obsession and the danger of loss of balance. The clichéd line, which exists because it is meaningful, is, "Don't lose your perspective. You're a cop. You have a responsibility to the law, the public." The warning is, of course, ignored.

7. *Following the trail.* The hero has to work his or her way through a cross section of society in an attempt to find or retrieve the criminal. The rich, the poor, bartenders, taxi drivers, rooming house owners, bums, and company presidents provide a chain of information that leads to . . .

8. *The second confrontation.* A direct, open, physical confrontation between the hero and the villain takes place in a hostile or an unfamiliar environment.

9. *The police officer destroys or captures the villain.* The strong tendency in television is not to destroy, however, but to capture, contain, and control the symbol of evil.

10. *The epilogue.* The second problem, that of the partner, is resolved. If the central problem is resolved violently, the secondary problem is usually resolved nonviolently. The resolution of the second problem can also take place during step 8. The criminal dealt with, the hero is either alone and shaken, or more often, taking the first steps toward returning to the partnership and balance.

Characters

In addition to the officer, the partner, and other officers, certain characters can be expected and developed:

Informers. Frequently the link turns out to be an unreliable mediator between the criminals and the police. Informers are usually not directly connected to the underworld. Generally they are comic-tragic figures on the fringes of two worlds, neither of which accepts them fully. The police officer, when dealing with the informer, must rely on skill and experience to determine the degree to which the informer can be used and trusted. An emotional connection usually exists or develops between the informer and the police officer.

Criminals. Strangely enough, television cops tend to be comfortable with criminals and in the criminal environment. This is the cop's manageable environment, something despised but understood. Often this attachment to the criminals and their world will be emphasized in an episode about the retirement of a uniformed cop. What will the cop do in retirement, removed from criminals, who have determined the meaning of his life? Retiring cuts the officer off from two important relationships: those with other police officers and those with criminals. Suicide often waits offscreen for the retiring or fired police officer. To lose the image of his dark side, to sever the connection to someone outside him who can take on all of his projections of evil, is devastating to the cop.

Middle-Class Representatives. Shopkeepers, small-business owners, and others—the very people the cop is most committed to protecting—are frequently encountered, though they remain the least defined characters in the tale. The cop's respect for them is usually evident, and his anger at those who refuse to cooperate with investigations is usually extreme because the cop feels betrayed.

Upper-Class Representatives. This is the social group to whom the police must be most deferential and with whom the police are least able to deal. The hero is uncomfortable and awkward with rich people, who represent a class and an environment based on wealth and power within which the police officer feels weak and helpless. The rich, professional upper classes are suspect in police tales because they are alien to the cop and, perhaps, alien and suspicious to the vast majority of viewers of the genre.

Family. A frequent irony in police tales is that the officer is unable to handle family members the way he or she can handle the criminal world or family difficulties encountered on the job—things the officer can control. Work is defined by rules and obligations. Families require an emotional flexibility that the police officer has trouble with. In television police tales home is where you go when no other place will take you and you simply can't work anymore.

Settings and Locations

Police tales are almost exclusively urban. This does not mean there are no stories about rural police officers and contemporary sheriffs, but on television the noncomic cop is generally an urban figure.

In dialogue and presentation, the city is presented as a potential jungle, a perverted primitive environment. The word *jungle* occurs repeatedly. As mentioned earlier, the cop is presented as a keeper of the law, a conformist, and conformity is needed to contain the animalism in the city. The beleaguered middle-class hero has no great intellectual capacity in this jungle but does possess a determination to save the city from the "animals."

Images and Tools of the Trade

The police officer has three primary tools that recur in the police tale on television—the gun, the uniform, and the vehicle.

The police officer typically has greater skill with a gun than does the criminal. Over the years, the handling of the gun has altered in police tales. Before Vietnam, the policeman stood, almost dispassionately, with his side to the target and the pistol at arm's length while he sighted down the barrel. Now the officer holds the gun with two hands and crouches, facing the target head-on. This has been universally accepted on television as the professional stance, the posture of training rather than that of the western gunfight.

Normally the gun is a symbol of order in the hands of a police officer. The officer has to be very careful not to abuse the gun. At the same time the gun represents the potential paranoia of the police officer, the ordinary person who has to make decisions all the time, to fire the gun or not fire it. In episode after episode an officer fires, shoots someone, and then has to go before a board of inquiry to justify why he fired. The cop's partner or partners must go out and find a bullet in an alley or someone who fired from a window to free and cleanse the officer of public guilt.

With a few exceptions, the "uniforms" of the detectives are nondescript. Their clothes are as inconspicuous as possible—not necessarily because they are hiding but because those are the clothes that they choose to wear. They dress as they are, lower-middle-class white-collar workers.

The antagonists, the bad guys, dress differently. Animalistic madmen, pimps, and petty criminals, because they are free of society's constraints, dress bizarrely. They have the freedom to be conspicuous. Successful organized-crime figures, however, usually dress the same as the cops, only better. They too wear clothing that is not conspicuous, but it is of far better quality—tailor-made suits rather than ones bought off the rack.

The automobile is the deadliest urban artifact in the police officer's domain. The police officer does not respect the vehicle. It is a hunk of interchangeable, expensive machinery that the cop gets a chance to use and display his or her skill. The car chase appears frequently in police tales to show the hero's mastery of the tools of his environment.

Other tools, like the two-way radio or the computer, represent the hero's access to technology, an access that suggests an institutional support system that is rarely available to the criminal.

The Police Story as Potential Tragedy

On television the police officer is presented as facing an overwhelming situation. It takes everything the officer has to keep up with it. Ultimately these tales, as I've suggested, are a kind of lower-middle-class potential tragedy. The police must suffer for society and risk their sanity, their lives, and even their loved ones.

One final important element that the writer should be aware of in working on police tales is their nonconclusive nature. While a criminal may be caught, it is usually suggested that the problem has not been solved. In private detective tales social order is usually restored, or a troubled or threatened individual is saved. In police tales the clear implication is that criminal activity never stops; it is only stemmed.

The Police Tale and Genre

This brief analysis of a specific genre indicates the kind of research and attention a writer must give not only to the specific series for which he or she wants to write but also to the broader elements of what that form has been, how it has evolved, and what people expect from it. It does not mean that the writer must provide the conventional, but to deviate from the conventional the writer must first understand it.

EXERCISE 10

—Following the analysis outlined in this chapter, write a treatment for a police series currently on television.

8

WRITING COMEDY
By Mark Walker

Many people question whether comedy writing for television can be taught to anyone but those who already have the necessary talent and therefore don't need instruction. To this somewhat tautological line of inquiry, I respond with a firmly equivocal "yes and no." In my opinion, if the answer to that important question were either a firm "yes" or a firm "no," much of what follows would be rendered too obvious to commit to paper or else pointless.

I am convinced that both talent and at least some instruction are necessary for anyone to launch a successful comedy-writing career in a reasonable amount of time. Other things are necessary too, such as some luck and persistence, and the initial chapters of this book have covered these factors very well. For the purposes of this chapter, though, I am going to offer to you what I consider the fundamentals, the mechanics, of writing comedy for television.

By this last sentence I do not mean to imply that I consider comedy writing a wholly mechanical process, that I will simply lay out a bunch of rules that when applied will allow anyone to crank out a salable script. There is no such batch of rules. But any art form (and, yes, I do consider writing for television an art) has boundaries, limitations, constraints. In this chapter I will describe, delineate, and discuss these limits. As elsewhere in the book, I will suggest a number of exercises that you should take very seriously; take the time to write them out and revise them.

Humor

In discussing comedy writing we cannot avoid some decidedly sticky questions: How does humor operate? What is humor? What kinds of arrangements of words on paper, when read or acted out, make people laugh?

Such noted thinkers as the philosopher Henri Bergson and Sigmund Freud have tackled this very question with results that may strike you as too reductive. Anyway, that's how their work strikes me. Too many jokes simply don't fit into the frameworks provided by these theorists. This chapter is not the place to delve deeply into the work of either man, but a very brief look may prove illuminating.

Suffice it to say that Bergson reduced humor to creative works in which mechanical processes interact with living beings in comical ways. But what about funny material that in no sensible way could be construed as, to use Bergson's phrase, "the mechanical encrusted upon the living"? Freud, on the other hand, reduced comedy to processes of the mind whereby the unconscious is tricked by disguised material (jokes) that if left undisguised would be censored by the unconscious, and laughter results as a kind of defense mechanism. What about jokes that the most prudish, meek person in the world would be hard pressed to deem offensive or threatening?

Any attempt to reduce comedy to such a specific theoretical formula would run into a similar problem—too many jokes cannot be explained by it. Another, more fundamental, problem is whether explaining jokes helps the creative process at all. Therefore, what I propose to do is to provide a descriptive—as opposed to theoretical—model of humor based upon viewers' expectations within the realm of television comedy.

Expectations

Expectations form a vital link between an audience and a television program or any other medium. People have very specific expectations of a certain show or a certain genre of show before they tune in. Although most people do not articulate them or even think about them very much, you, as a writer, should be aware that an audience expects certain things from comedy on television.

We can analyze this facet of television writing on two different levels. First we can examine expectations on an individual show basis. Or we can look at this phenomenon over the run of a show or genre of shows. Let's first take a look at how expectations operate in television on a show-by-show basis.

Humor and Expectations

No matter what form of comedy writing you want to do for television, and we'll discuss several different forms in a little while, certain things can be said that apply equally to all expectations of humor. Nearly all comedy writing involves playing with expectations and the unexpected. In other words, regarding television comedy you can expect your audience to expect a great deal of the unexpected. For purposes of analysis, I will break these down into three categories: unexpected visuals, unexpected actions, and unexpected language.

UNEXPECTED VISUALS

This category is perhaps the simplest one to define and to discuss. Unexpected visuals, or "sight gags," can be defined as comedic visuals that happen on the periphery of the main action of a scene. The history of television comedy is rife with examples, and you can probably come up with many off the top of your head. To illustrate I'll briefly mention just three.

For instance, who could forget the eerie dream episode of *The Dick Van Dyke Show* when at one point thousands of walnuts come cascading out of one of the Petrie family's closets? How about Lucy's fling at stomping grapes at a small winery on *I Love Lucy*? Or how about Jethro Bodine's triumphant entrance in *The Beverly Hillbillies* as "Agent Double-Naught Seven," when he was decked out in a trench coat bulging with special "Naught-Naught" gadgets?

UNEXPECTED ACTIONS

Another broad category includes unexpected actions, which are somewhat similar to sight gags except that these comedic actions form the main actions of a scene or segment without recourse to dialogue. Thus, funny sounds apart from spoken language would fall into this category.

For instance, in one episode of *The Honeymooners* Ralph decides to pick up some spare cash by becoming the super of his apartment building. When things go on the fritz in the basement, Ralph tries to repair things himself and gets hopelessly stuck in the heating pipes while doing to.

Similarly, on *I Love Lucy,* Lucy Ricardo decides to take a job at a chocolate factory to make some extra money. In one of the best-known scenes in television, she struggles desperately as the conveyor belt containing the candies she must finish careens out of control. As tray upon tray of candy hits the floor and she gives up in frustration, her boss of just a few minutes walks in to check her progress.

The comedy writer must walk the line between the expected and the unexpected. That is, part of the reason that these bits work so well is this very dichotomy between the expected and the unexpected. Ralph and Lucy are constantly doing similar things to get themselves into trouble, but not precisely the same thing. The writers of these episodes have given a familiar situation a funny twist.

Consider the following twists on the two comedic actions described above:

Ralph cannot get out from in between the pipes. No one knows where he went, and after a while he dies. Would audiences find this development funny? Probably not. The reaction would more likely have been anger, even outrage. People would feel cheated, tricked, let down. Clearly, audience expectations are not infinitely elastic.

Or, on a less dramatic note, imagine Bea Arthur's character Maude taking the job that Lucy took. Would the scene play as well as the original without major changes? I don't think so. Maude probably would have hauled back and slugged the boss.

Interestingly enough, the conveyor belt scene has been remade, on one of the early *Saturday Night Live* shows. Gilda Radner, playing the Lucy role, gets a job working at a defense plant. She goes through the same travail as did her predecessor, although in this case the stakes are considerably higher—the candies have been replaced by nuclear weapons. The scene ends with the destruction of a good part of the world. Given the counterexample of the death of Ralph Kramden, how can this sketch have been played for comedy? Well, the Not Ready for

Prime Time Players have taken the expected/ unexpected dichotomy one step further, have added an additional twist. They are playing with the conventions of narrative comedy on television, one of which is that such serious topics as nuclear annihilation are almost never a comedic subject in this realm. Also, the context of the late night show—out of prime time, striving to be hip, irreverent, etc.—should be taken into consideration. I will discuss such contexts in greater detail later in this chapter.

UNEXPECTED LANGUAGE—COMEDIC DIALOGUE

We now move on to a vital component of comedy writing, unexpected language. There are two ways of considering comedic dialogue unexpected. First, writing in this form basically deviates from what you strive for in most kinds of dramatic writing, an illusion of reality. Also, much of the language in television comedy can be seen as giving verbal form to the sight gags and unexpected actions considered above. Let's examine each of these ways in turn.

Television comedy writing strives for only the most limited illusion of reality in terms of dialogue. Even in the shows more lauded for their realism—*All in the Family, M*A*S*H, Mary Tyler Moore*—the language is extremely heightened, and I suspect most people consider these shows realistic due to their wonderfully well-rounded characters. As separating characters from their dialogue always distorts things, let's just say that beginning writers should not immediately strive to create both highly realistic and funny dialogue at the same time. One of these elements will surely suffer.

Anyway, by saying that the language in these shows is heightened and often not particularly realistic, I do not mean at all that I consider this a shortcoming. Quite the contrary, I think you should study these shows very carefully if you are serious about becoming a comedy writer. You should also look at shows not particularly noted for their realism—for example, *Happy Days, ALF, Perfect Strangers, I Love Lucy*—and compare these to the ones noted above.

But if striving for an illusion of reality in television comedy is what you want to do, don't do it primarily in your dialogue. Why not? Look at it this way. The kinds of things that are virtues in most television drama, the things that create the illusion of reality in dialogue, are anathema in television comedy. Small talk, trailing-off thoughts, repetition, picking up other people's thoughts, etc., will deaden your script unless you're clever enough to make jokes nearly every time you use one of these techniques.

And you have to make a lot of jokes. Really a lot of jokes.

Harlan Ellison:

"Sitcoms need a laugh every third line: your beat line, your setup line, and then your ha-ha line."

The norm in half-hour comedies seems to be about two jokes per page, about three per minute. Have you ever met someone who told three jokes a minute and kept it up, even for a half hour? I hope not, for your sake. The point is, what's improbable, even very annoying, in real life is standard and even laudatory in half-hour comedy.

EXERCISE **11**

Pick a comedy you consider fairly realistic. Count the jokes. Pick another comedy, one that you don't consider realistic. Count the jokes again. Is there a difference? in number? in kind?

Speaking of kinds of jokes, regarding television comedy dialogue I would classify them this way: one-liners, witticisms, comebacks, stingers, and even the occasional pun and riddle. These types of jokes can be described according to the work they do within the context of a scene:

■ **A one-liner,** as the term implies, is a short gag in which the joke remains intact even if said out of context of the scene.

■ **A witticism** is a comic observation about the state of things, sometimes said as a throwaway (or an aside), not always in direct response to what is happening in the scene.

■ **A comeback** is a comic retort to something someone has said and can often be hostile.

■ Finally, a **stinger** is a joke at the end of an act or a major scene. Stingers have to be strong jokes and have to do a lot of work. Basically, they have to rehook the viewers and make them want to stick around for the next scene (see Chapter Three).

These joke forms are listed for your convenience only. If you come up with jokes that don't easily fit into one of these categories, don't go overboard. By all means use it, as long as it fits in sensibly with your script. These forms are listed to get you thinking about different forms of jokes used in TV and how you might use them.

Another way to look at jokes in television comedy is to group them a little more broadly, again using expectations as a basis of comparison. Verbal jokes play with conventions and with expectations of them as much as do the visual ones described above. Other jokes play with expectations in other ways, such as through exaggeration and comic juxtaposition of ideas. Since it makes little sense to list examples of verbal jokes out of their contexts, I'll leave the gathering of examples to you.

EXERCISE 12

—Watch, preferably tape, a half-hour comedy and do the following: Classify the jokes. Are there comebacks? witticisms? one-liners? stingers? How can the jokes be said to be playing with expectations? Are there any jokes based upon exaggeration? juxtaposition of ideas?

Genres of Television Comedy

The two broad categories of shows of interest to us are the narrative comedy and the variety show. The former is often called the "situation" comedy, but that term is so broad as to be now almost meaningless. I will break down narrative comedy into four different genres, more usable categories, in a moment.

THE VARIETY SHOW

The Milton Berle Show, The Ed Sullivan Show, Saturday Night Live, Fridays, Second City Television, The Tracy Ullman Show, and *Dolly* are good examples of the variety show. They are nonnarrative forms on television featuring various kinds of acts: music, magic, animals, and comedy. The comedy itself can take the form of stand-up material, sketches, and blackouts. As you might surmise from the list above, the comedy-variety show is not in great vogue at the moment. With the exception of *Saturday Night Live, The Tracy Ullman show,* and *Dolly,* all those shows have become a part of TV history.

That fact in turn might imply that the market for writing for such shows is nonexistent. That's not quite true. There is a market, but it's small and hard to crack. The few shows remaining have large staffs working to satisfy the demand for material. With so few comedy-variety shows in production it's an open question as to how long even that small market will remain viable. Still, there is a cousin of the variety show that seems to be going strong on television at present. This form is the talk show.

While the market for this type of show is small as well, it is perhaps worth considering before we turn our attention to the forms of narrative comedy for the rest of the chapter. *Late Night with David Letterman, The Tonight Show, The Late Show,* and the others need to employ staffs as well, to provide for their almost daily need for material. More information about approaching these markets can be found in Chapter Eleven.

Narrative Comedy

The more traditional route, as detailed in Chapter Four, is to write a spec script to show that you know how to write on an extended basis. This brings us into the realm of narrative comedy. A sketch or a couple of one-liners cannot be as much a showcase for your writing as can the sustained job of a completed narrative script. This supercategory can more helpfully be broken down into four types, as Stuart Kaminsky points out in another book of his, *American Television Genres*. These four are the individual, the courtship, the institutional, and the family comedies. These forms are fluid. That is, a particular show can be said to have characteristics of more than one of these types. It is not necessary to go into great detail here about these four types of narrative comedy; just a few details and examples from them should help steer you toward the type of writing you'll feel most comfortable with or help you refine the writing you're doing now.

The Individual Comedy. This type centers around a lone, usually a childish person. The protagonist here often goes to comic extremes to avoid growing up and the attendant responsibilities of adulthood. This type is not very popular at the present, but classic examples include *I Love Lucy* and *The Honeymooners*.

The Courtship Comedy. The primary conflict in this type comes from the inexperience of one of two main characters in matters of romance. Traditionally, the male character appears as the one who lacks the romantic experience. The early *Rhoda* shows (before Rhoda got married), *Duet,* and *Cheers* fall into this category.

The Institutional Comedy. This type revolves around a group of people, usually in a workplace. The major problem facing the characters in this type of comedy comes from the interpersonal relationships found among the group. Tensions arise among the members of the group as they cope with day-to-day living. *M*A*S*H* and *Head of the Class* are examples of institutional comedies.

The Family Comedies. From *Father Knows Best* to *The Cosby Show,* these comedies draw their main source of conflict from the problems of characters trying to act responsibly toward one another. Often the specific crisis for a particular show is a failure on the part of one of the family members to act in the interests of the others. Then that character confesses the shortcoming to resolve the crisis of the week. Throughout TV history, this role has again and again fallen to the father, but in your writing the specific nature of conflict and resolution is, of course, your decision.

The reason for listing types of narrative comedy in television history is not a prescriptive one, nor do I mean to help you on the pink questions in Trivial Pursuit. That is to say, I do not mean to imply that you must follow these forms to write television comedy, but knowledge of them can help you a lot. These are descriptive forms. Since audiences are quite familiar with them and have formed their expectations in line with them, you should be familiar with them too. How far you intend to deviate from the forms or how closely you would like to keep to them is a decision you must make on your own. But you should be aware that they exist and of what forms you feel most comfortable with.

Characters and Situations

It is often repeated that the humor from "good" television comedy springs from well-crafted, "real" characters. To a great extent I agree with that statement, as long as the situations in which these carefully wrought characters find themselves are not neglected. If you don't give these characters interesting actions as well as clever, funny dialogue, you'll be throwing out the baby (as well as the mama and the papa, if you're writing a family comedy) with the bathwater.

Situations are more than just locales; they are also the predicaments that your characters find themselves in. Also, characters are more than just what they say; they are also to a great extent what they do. Therefore, character and situation must work together in a tightly written television comedy.

Larry Gelbart:

"If you can come up with some really wonderful situation that is a filter through which even already established characters can operate, then you can demonstrate something to the producers of an established show."

In other words, if you can add jokes to a sound script structure in which, say, the characters from *Family Ties* interact in an extremely clever situation, you've got a spec script you can show around with confidence. All these elements are necessary. Let's turn now to a bit more detailed discussion of character and situation. We'll separate them briefly for purposes of analysis.

As to the specific types of characters with which comedy

scripts are populated, let's look back at the four types of narrative comedy. The individual comedy contains a childlike or at least childish character who is trying to avoid responsibility. The courtship comedy, say, *Cheers,* portrays two or more dating characters involved in a relationship. The institutional comedy shows a group of characters, *WKRP in Cincinnati* and *Designing Women* for instance, trying to get along in an institutional setting. Finally, the family comedy, from *Leave It to Beaver* to *Family Ties* and *Married: With Children* contains a family unit, characters dealing with family problems.

As you can see, the genre classification is at least partially drawn from the characters found in any particular show within a genre. Conversely, the genre in which you choose to write determines at the very least the major characters you choose to write about. The treatment of those major characters becomes the place that you can show your talent as a writer. Further, the generic description hints at the situation, at least in a general way.

Since you as a beginning writer will probably be first writing spec scripts, your options for handling characters are somewhat limited. That is, you should not introduce a major character change in your spec scripts. For example, having the Huxtables of *The Cosby Show,* basically a family comedy, go through a messy divorce would probably be a bad idea. Similarly, having the entire class from the institutional comedy *Head of the Class* graduate in your spec script is probably more of a change than most producers would like to undergo. You should be watching very closely the forms that you wish to emulate, timing them and taking notes.

Garry Marshall:

"There are certain formulas, but not too many general ones, that include all shows. Each show seems to have its own formula, and each shop has its own formula. You have to be aware that to write for the Norman Lear organization was totally different from writing for the Garry Marshall organization or writing for the Aaron Spelling shop or writing for Larry Gelbart. Each guy dictates his own style and the way he wants his show done. If you don't want to do it that way, don't come. Once in a while you'd get someone who'd be better over at Jim Brooks, so I'd recommend him. It's not an adversarial relationship. Norman Lear has sent writers to me. It would help if the writer himself could tell the difference. But sometimes they don't understand it; they think it's all the same.''

EXERCISE 13

—Tape a half-hour comedy that you have never seen before and watch exactly fifteen minutes of it. Stop watching at this point and finish the script on your own. Watch the rest of the show and compare versions. Did you write similar actions occurring at similar times? If not, why not?

EXERCISE 14

—Pick a half-hour comedy that you like and study its form. How frequent are the jokes? How quickly has the hook been set? At what point did you know who the major character was going to be? How quickly was the initial problem set up? the secondary problem? What are the stingers of the script? Where are they found? What production company puts out this show? Is this show typical of that production company?

You should notice that practically none of the valuable twenty-three to twenty-four minutes (roughly thirty to forty pages of formatted script; see Chapters Three and Four) of an established show is given up to exposition about characters. In the rare instances that this is done, it is almost always used as a joke, a beat, a problem, or a stinger. Still, it is almost uncanny that even casual watchers of television have more information about shows than is ever given in the body of the program. How is this information conveyed?

In a number of ways. Many programs (*Newhart, The Beverly Hillbillies, Laverne and Shirley, Green Acres, The Odd Couple, ALF, Head of the Class*) have opening sequences that provide a lot of information about what the characters have done in the past. Also, we receive lots of information about TV characters from sources completely apart from the shows themselves. These include other TV shows, newspaper reviews, TV listings, commercials, other people, even articles of clothing that come and go from fashion. In other words, we all receive a lot more information about things like TV shows from the surrounding culture than we usually think we do.

The main point is that you have to know what is important to include about your characters and what is important to leave out. In most cases you don't have room to pursue character history in your scripts. You should think of script space as very valuable; everything you put in the script should earn its spot.

Another thing you have to do is to make sure your characters have ongoing appeal.

Garry Marshall:

"In series television the actors have got to be on every week. So you have got to write them a little likable, because what you're doing is asking people to let these actors into their house. And nobody wants despicable people in their house."

Here the writer must walk another tightrope, making the characters likable on the one hand and keeping audiences feeling a bit superior to them on the other. This is because it is much easier to elicit laughter when your audience feels superior to your creations, your characters. Depending upon what genre you choose to tackle and what specific shows you use as models, you can attempt to channel audience identification in various ways. This is addressed in much more detail in Chapter Three. Keeping this discussion on the level of viewer projections onto character, you can attempt this by making your characters childish in an individual comedy, inexperienced in romantic affairs in a courtship show, crabby at work in an institutional comedy, irresponsible around the house on a family show, and so on.

Remember, you're doing all this in a context, a situation determined by characters, jokes, and story structure. It is not easy to isolate any of these in practice. If any of these can be separated out, you haven't written a tightly structured script, and whatever is excess should be cut. When you're writing you've got to keep all these plates spinning, balls juggling—you name the cliché—at once.

Since this brief discussion of characters and situations is geared toward getting you to write a professional spec script, the next exercise is inevitable.

EXERCISE 15

Write a spec script for a half-hour comedy show using what you have learned so far in this chapter.

Audiences

If you've done the exercises to this point, you have already done some comedy writing. How do you know it's funny? You have to test it on an audience. What kind of audience?

You naturally would like to reach as wide an audience as possible on either network or cable TV. Along the way toward your ultimate goal, though, there are usually at least a couple of other audiences to consider. For instance, if you attract the

attention of a producer with a spec script, you will almost
certainly have to pitch further stories to him or her as described
in Chapter Twelve.

Garry Marshall:

"I think to be able to make someone laugh in the comedy field is very
important. So I think pitching in comedy is critical because if you can make the
person laugh when pitching him, he will figure you might be a good writer."

In addition, it is not a bad idea to try out your material on a
few other people before you try to get to the pitching stage. One
way to have an audience is to build one into the writing stage—
write with a partner. I often collaborate when writing comedy
and have found it a good method to try out jokes at a very early
point in the progress.

Bob Shayne:

"I was half of a team for about three years when I first started, and it seems
like a lot of writers, especially in comedy, start out as teams. In many cases,
each of the members of the team gets proficient enough to do it on his own.
Then they split up."

Bill Nuss:

"There aren't many people who, like Neil Simon, can sit down in a dark room
and come up with twenty-four minutes of solid jokes."

Garry Marshall:

"Collaboration seems to work best on comedy because you have someone to
bounce the humor off of. It makes, I think, for better scripts. Two people
working together doesn't necessarily make better jokes; they just eliminate the
worst jokes."

It can also be a lot of fun.

It can be good experience as well, for if you reach the level of the networks, you will need to function effectively with other writers at a wide variety of meetings and sessions.

Bob Shayne:

"But then there's a larger kind of collaboration that happens when the individual writer or writing team is hired by a bunch of producer/writers, story editor/writers who function on a TV series. You've got to put up with these people, especially if it's on a series. It's their series. They run it. They own it. They think they understand it. And they're going to be right. When you get into a story meeting or script meeting room, you'll be with four, five, or six writers, most of whom are on the staff.

"The dynamics of that situation dictate that the free-lance writer will throw out an idea and somebody in the room will contradict it."

Bill Nuss:

"Television comedy is very collaborative in that a script is written by one writer, then goes to the table, where the writers sit around and work on the script, breaking it down and punching it up in terms of jokes. It's much more of a contribution by each staff member when the final product hits the taping stage in front of an audience. The script has undergone a big change in the course of a week, and everybody who is on the writing staff has contributed to that."

Larry Gelbart:

"There is a lot of collaboration. Some of it goes on without your being part of it. There isn't a series that doesn't take outsider writers' work or even staff writers' work and rework it constantly."

If you don't feel comfortable writing with others, there are a number of other ways you can test your material before audiences, ranging from the very small to very large, depending on your inclination:

■ You can pitch some of your jokes or even story ideas to the people around the proverbial water cooler at work, to people you go to school with, to your family, to people you see socially, to anyone you feel comfortable talking to. If you need to build up your confidence, start with a smaller number of people and try to work your way up to larger numbers.

■ If you're not shy at all, you can take to the stage at open-mike night at a local nightclub or bar if there's one convenient to you. Some colleges and community groups have open mikes and talent nights that are open to the public as well. If you're not ready for the footlights there, you can always try to get your material to someone willing to perform at one of these venues.

■ You can also try to get your material to local/cable talk and variety shows. There is some more information about this process in Chapter Eleven.

■ Finally, there are also screenwriting classes and writers' workshops where you can try out your material on a real live audience and sometimes get class members to do readings for you. If this is a major reason for your enrollment, be sure to check with the instructor before signing up. Make sure the course offers what you want it to.

Remember, in comedy every audience counts.

CHAPTER

9

WRITING MADE-FOR-TELEVISION MOVIES AND MINISERIES

Made-for-Television Movies

The market for made-for-television movies is a good and a bad one. It is good because since the early 1960s there have been regular time slots on every network for feature films. Today the major cable networks also devote a significant part of their budgets to producing feature films primarily for cable. In short, the market does not look as if it is going away.

Another primary advantage of the made-for-television market is that it allows you greater flexibility in subject matter and doesn't, as series television does, tie you into specific genres, situations, and characters. CBS, NBC, and ABC are interested in films that they might turn into regular series, but series potential need not be the deciding factor in a sale. In fact, often the networks will make it clear that they do *not* want made-for-television films that are series pilots. You'll find out which is the case as you start submitting scripts. Cable networks, primarily HBO and Showtime, have even less interest in producing films that might serve as series pilots. Another possible advantage of writing a movie for cable is that you can use subjects, language, and images that would give you an R rating in theatrical release. For the networks you are generally working on films that would earn a PG or PG-13 rating.

A primary disadvantage to the beginner writing the made-for-television movie is the competition and the need for reputation. Networks seldom entertain a proposal or pitch from an unknown writer for a made-for-television movie. Generally proposals and pitches for made-for-television movies come from producers who have a record of some success in the field, producers who have some credits, producers who might be able to put together a package, not just a project. The package might include script, star or stars, and director.

Then how do you break in if you have a script?

First, write the script. It's a risk. You might not be able to find a producer who will look at it, but it is the way to start. A good way to get that producer or agent to look at your first made-for-television movie script is to base it on a known project—a historical event or character, a play or novel now in the public domain. Don't—I repeat, don't—write a proposal or treatment or script for a film based on a project that you do not have the rights to. It is simple enough to check with your local library to find out if an old novel or play is in the public domain. If it is not, you must obtain the rights from either the author or the estate of the author before you write. Normally to obtain such rights you indicate to the author that you are willing to pay a fixed amount, an option, for that property for a given period of time.

A common practice for a producer/screenwriter is to obtain the rights to a novel or a play for one year with an option to renew for an additional year or six months at an agreed-upon fee. If you are talking about a fairly obscure novel, it is reasonable to offer as little as $2,500 or even less for that first year and the same amount or less for each additional year. The option contract usually includes an agreement that if the script is sold for production the novelist or playwright of the original work will be given credit—"from the novel by . . . ," "based on the novel . . . by . . ."—and will be given another payment for the right to use that work. The contract may also call for the original author to receive a percentage of the production cost, net or gross earnings of the film if it is given theatrical release. Remember, the option does not give you the rights to that work. The option gives you the right to prepare the script and try to find someone who will buy the project. If you fail to sell the project and your script by the end of the option period, you must renew your option or you will lose all rights to that property.

Obviously, the details of the above are a bit beyond the interests or ability of most would-be or professional television writers. The answer, once again, is to have an agent (see Chapter Eleven). So, I suggest that before you start considering obtaining the rights to that book you love, particularly if it is a major novel that might require option money of more than $50,000 a year, you come up with a far less ambitious first project for your made-for-television movie.

All right, if you don't go for an adaptation of a major work you would have to option, what can you do? *If you intend to follow any of the following options, please consult your attorney regarding the particulars.*

■ Base your script on a work in the public domain. Variations and modernizations of Shakespeare and Dumas appear frequently on television not only because the authors are popular but also because their works are free to any writer who wishes to use them. The same thing is true of characters if the rights to those characters have run out. Sherlock Holmes's popularity as a film and television figure is based strongly on the fact that anyone may now write a Holmes story without paying the Conan Doyle estate. Film scripts based on classical tales are not only a good way for you to learn; they also offer the possibility of selling a script based on a known work or character without any subsidiary costs to you. The problem, and there always is one, is that you will not be the only person to think of or know this, but that's no reason to refrain from doing it. Your goal is to write a script that will attract the attention of a reputable agent.

■ Base your script on a public figure. Public figures, such as Frank Sinatra, Elizabeth Taylor, and Richard Nixon, among others, are in the public domain. You can't commit slander, but you can fictionalize the lives of famous people, though it is usually safer to fictionalize the lives of dead public figures. Fictionalized accounts of the lives of Al Capone, Douglas Mac-Arthur, Clark Gable, W. C. Fields, Woody Guthrie, and hundreds of others have been produced. Again, no money need be paid to the estates of these public figures. If you can find an interesting public figure and, through research, come up with an incident or incidents in their lives that would be the basis of a dramatic tale, make the proposal and write the script. I know, for example, that made-for-television scripts are currently being written about Alfred Hitchcock, Groucho Marx, and General William Westmoreland. You might just get lucky and send your script to an agent who represents an actor who would love to play the character you have based your script on.

■ Base your script on a contemporary news event. If you do that, however, you have to be prepared to write quickly. You won't be the only one with the idea. The trick is to see the drama in a news event in which others might not see the drama. The Iran/Contra Senate hearings formed the basis for several scripts. News stories about child abuse, wife beating, AIDS, homosexuality, and mass murderers have all been material for made-for-television movies. Occasionally, particularly in cases in which someone has achieved celebrity status and is officially cooperating on a film or television version of the news event, it might be a good idea to base your script on the event but not present the script as a fictionalizing of the specific event. For example, you might want to write a made-for-television script about an Oliver North–type military officer who gets in trouble, possibly even goes to prison, for taking on a task he convinces himself is desired by the president of the United States.

Prepare the made-for-television script as you would any television script as indicated earlier in this book? Please refer to Chapter Three for suggestions about script structure.

Some suggestions about preparing the made-for-television script:

■ If it is your first made-for-television project, keep your idea basic and straightforward and make sure it could be done reasonably and inexpensively. It might be a good idea in a first script to keep the number of characters and locations down—perhaps no more than five or six major characters and five or six primary locations.

■ Don't tie your first script into difficult terrain or seasonal problems—snowstorms, jungle rain forests.

■ Before you write a word, watch and study made-for-television movies. Time them. See where the act breaks come and what happens just before and after the breaks. Write down the number of characters, major and minor, and identify the locations. If you can tape the movie and look at it several times, see how long it takes to introduce the characters and the problem. What are the primary and secondary problems? Are there additional problems? What is the problem of each of the major characters, and how are these problems solved or resolved? What is done to attract immediate viewer interest? After the primary problem is solved, how are other problems resolved? How much time is devoted to the postresolution story, the story after the problem has essentially been solved? What happens in this postresolution part of the tale?

Be sure to prepare a brief summary of the script and a treatment. And be sure to make use of what you have learned and practiced about story, character, and dialogue in previous chapters. A good idea is essential to get the attention of an agent or producer for a made-for-television movie. To hold that attention you need striking character and dialogue and a story told in beats that lead up to acts that end with questions and climaxes.

ADAPTATION

Since adaptation can be an important part of writing made-for-television movies or, for that matter, miniseries, a few suggestions might help you when adapting a novel, a nonfiction book, or a play for television.

If you've written a script for a feature film before, remember that there are important differences between features and made-for-TV movies.

Garry Marshall:

"Artistically in TV, no matter what you do, unless you're writing for PBS, you have to write with a bit of an eye toward a mass audience. In films you can write to a select group. You can write an 'art house' film. In prime time television there seems to be no 'art house' slot. It's all mass appeal. So, you just have to be intelligent enough to say 'This is the kind of work I like to do' and find a place where your work is appreciated.

"On the business end, television pays better. It's more consistent. In movies it takes forever; sometimes you don't get the real money until the picture is shot. In TV you always get paid."

Bill Nuss:

"One difference is that things get made. TV is much faster and things get made. You see what you write. There are people that spend a lot of time writing movies. There aren't as many movies that get made as there are TV shows that get made."

Jeff Rice:

"Television's produced 'on the cheap' compared to big-screen films (although, with some hour-long series budgeted at $1 million per episode, *cheap* is a relative term), and there is very little time to set up well-thought-out visuals and set up an overall mood. You deal in seconds instead of minutes. It's like a comic book compared to the original movie or like the *Reader's Digest* version of a full novel."

Bob Shayne:

"I don't think it's all that different from writing for movies except that you don't have all the special effects and that you have to limit the sets and characters. Obviously, it is less visual by far than a large-budget adventure kind of theatrical movie."

Also, recognize that books and television scripts are radically different and address quite different things. A novel, for example, can be any length from a hundred to a thousand pages or more. Your script must be far shorter than even a very short novel. Something's got to give; something's got to be cut from the novel. Your dilemma stems from the frequent belief that your goal as adapter is to be "true to the original." That is not only a difficult task; it is an impossible one. You can be true only to your belief in what the novel means. Adaptation requires decisions, cutting, and change. What might be perfectly reasonable, even essential, in a novel may be impossible in a film. For example, here is the opening paragraph of my novel *When the Dark Man Calls:*

Crickets, millions of them, made the hot summer night cry in the woods behind the house, but Jean hardly noticed. From her bed she could see deep into the trees where the fireflies, twinkling like stars, turned the darkness into a mock sky, her private sky. She lay unwilling to remove the protection of the no-longer-cool sheet. A slight breeze puffed through the window, not sufficient to make the drapes billow, but enough to make a daddy longlegs pause and lower its body against the window ledge.

This paragraph typifies the problems the sceenwriters faced as they adapted the novel. The information is presented from the perspective of a ten-year-old girl. The script can indicate that we see her, but how are we to know how she feels? We can see how she acts and reacts, but the film cannot give us access to her thoughts, sensations. The film or teleplay can *show* characters, but it cannot penetrate them. That is both the advantage and the disadvantage of a film over a novel or a short story. The film can show. The novel cannot. The novel can get into the feelings and sensations of a character. The film cannot.

Let's look at the specific problems of adapting that one paragraph, assuming you wanted somehow to include that opening paragraph in your screenplay

We can certainly show the woods:

1. EXT. WOODS OUTSIDE CARRBORO, NORTH CAROLINA. NIGHT.

But what do we do next? Do we show crickets? Do we try to show "millions" of crickets? Wouldn't that be a distortion of the paragraph and distract from the little girl, Jean, in the room? Should we simply hear the sound of crickets and move right into the room?

1. EXT. WOODS OUTSIDE CARRBORO, NORTH CAROLINA. NIGHT.
The sound of CRICKETS, thousands of crickets.
2. EXT. KAISER HOUSE. NIGHT.
The sound of CRICKETS continues. A slight wind billows the curtains in a second-floor window.
3. INT. JEAN KAISER'S ROOM. NIGHT.
JEAN is in her bed. The CRICKETS continue, but their sound fades.

Problem: Does saying or showing "their sound fades" convey the idea in the novel that "Jean hardly notices"?

The problems continue. How do we show in a script and subsequent film that the fireflies turn "the darkness into a mock sky, her private sky"? We can't show it. We might want to suggest it with a look on her face, but what kind of look? It goes on. How do we show that she is "unwilling to remove the protection of the no-longer-cool sheet"? How do we know that the sheet was once cool?

We can simply skip the paragraph and go on to the next, but it gets no easier. In adapting, you must constantly make decisions about what you can and cannot do and what, in your opinion, makes the most dramatic or appropriate image and action. This often means that the novel is stripped to its surface, the things people say and do and the places in which they are done. Introspection vanishes or, dangerously, has to be turned into dialogue. The danger of turning feelings and thoughts into dialogue is that it slows your story, not to mention that it is not really a way of preserving what you think is the essence of the original. Converting the novel to a teleplay and trying to retain the thoughts and feelings by turning them into dialogue is actually a disservice to the original work.

So you make decisions which turn the original text—novel, play, nonfiction book—into an outline, a suggestion, rather than a text that has to be faithfully and magically turned into a script.

The result, always, is that the book and the film are quite different. They have to be.

Garner Simmons:

"They're just totally like apples and oranges. A novelist can get inside the character's head, something that is not very well effected in television. If you watch *Spenser: For Hire,* there's a lot of voice-over narration that sort of parallels things you'd get out of a novel. But in reality you have a minimal amount of time to get down on paper and later on the screen what you would be able to do over hundreds of pages in a novel. In a novel you can spend ten pages describing one side of a room. You do not have the same situation in television.''

Comparing books and made-for-television films or miniseries may be interesting, but the really fruitful point for the writer is what decisions were made and why. How might you do it differently?

No two writers will adapt a novel in the same way. That doesn't mean that one is right and one is wrong. It may be that the two have different approaches to the original, different elements that they see as dramatic and important.

EXERCISE 16

—Take a recent favorite novel and write a treatment for converting it to a made-for-television movie. Indicate what you would remove and why. Where would you begin? What would your seven acts be?

A final thought on adapting for television: Consider writing your own novel. It may well be that a reasonable entrée to television or film is not always by first writing the spec script, series, or adaptation but by writing a novel and, in the back of your mind, hoping that it will be considered for film or television and that you will have sufficient power to ensure that you will be involved in the writing of that script.

The market for first novels is not terribly good either, but it may offer some advantages over trying to break into the television-writing market. It is easier to get a literary agent who will take a serious look at your novel than it is to get a media agent to look at your script. An added irony is that if your novel does make it to television, you'll make far more money by having written it as a novel that must be purchased for adaptation than if you wrote the story as an original script.

The Miniseries

The miniseries is a far more difficult market to break into than series television or made-for-television movies. The reasons are fairly obvious. Few miniseries are put into production. Those that are produced are almost always the work of major producers—Wolper, Lorimar, Paramount—and the vast majority of produced miniseries are based on major biographies, novels, or nonfiction books.

The chances of a new writer proposing or being assigned to write a miniseries are very slim, but there are a few things you can do to help if that is your goal.

The primary thing to do is come up with an idea for a miniseries that hasn't been done and to get that idea to a producer who has a proven record in miniseries. Go through *Variety* or go to the library and get a book on television credits. There are several such books. Find out who has produced miniseries and, when you get your idea together, submit your treatment, ideally through an agent, to that producer.

In this case, your treatment should be substantial, twenty-five pages at least, in which you indicate what the acts and scenes of the finished script would include. My treatment for the feature *Shepard's Tower* is twenty-five pages, and that is for a script of a hundred pages, approximately a ninety-minute feature. The treatment for the feature film *Once Upon a Time in America* is more than a hundred pages for a film with a running time of three hours and forty minutes.

Assuming each episode of a miniseries fits into a two-hour time slot, each episode should run about 120 script pages and be divided into acts in much the same way the made-for-television film is divided into acts (see Chapter Three). An important difference is that I suggest each episode of a miniseries end with an important secondary problem solved and the major problem unsolved.

Ideas for miniseries should be the reverse, generally, of made-for-television movies. Miniseries ideas, because of the time commitment by the network, have a suggestion of the grand or monumental. They deal with major crimes (*Fatal Vision, Helter Skelter*), epic tales (*Centennial, North and South*), major historical events (*Washington Behind Closed Doors, The Missiles of October*), vast imaginative landscapes (*Amerika, V, The Martian Chronicles, Space*), or multigenerational sagas (*Roots, Chiefs*).

So, what hasn't been done? A remake of *Birth of a Nation* evoking D. W. Griffith's scenes and characters but telling the tale from the perspective of the slaves and former slaves and not the Ku Klux Klan? How about a series on Teddy Roosevelt?

EXERCISE 17

—Go the library, spend an evening browsing, and come up with at least five good ideas for miniseries, including a multigenerational tale, a historical tale, an epic tale, and an imaginative tale with a broad landscape.

10

WRITING THE DOCUMENTARY

There are many kinds of documentary, some of which are written to match footage already shot and some of which are conceived and written before production begins. Before examining each of those in turn, let's take a look at strategies for generating salable documentary ideas.

Coming Up with Documentary Ideas

Television like *60 Minutes* and *20/20* can produce documentaries quickly and deal with current news and tie-ins. The novice documentary writer has to come up with ideas that may be timely but will not be dated by the passage of a news story from the public consciousness.

Ongoing problems, continuing public figures, ideas that have a seasonal or an event tie-in are all open to the documentary writer. For example:

Ongoing problems—how hospitals take care of dying patients, missing children, parents who fail to pay child support, the high cost of going to college.

Continuing public figures—What happened to Greta Garbo?, retired presidents, What do ex-athletes do when they retire?, athletes who have entered politics, show business people in politics.

Seasonal or event tie-ins—Trick or Treat: Is Halloween too dangerous to continue?, the men who play Santa Claus once a year, the forgotten soldiers of Memorial Day, a woman who is facing great odds in her run for public office.

Granted, many of the ideas above would not get very far, but they give you the idea.

Another important consideration, however, is that the subject chosen should have visual possibilities. The Greta Garbo idea relies on getting the right to use clips of Garbo films and the hope that new footage of Garbo will be obtainable. The woman facing odds in running for office offers the possibility of following her to events and watching her in her nonpolitical life. Parents who fail to pay child support sounds like a good idea, but the visual possibilities might be too limited. It might be difficult to find and get permission to interview the nonpaying parents. You might wind up with talking heads, head shots of people being interviewed, which are normally not of sufficient audience interest to sustain more than a small percentage of the documentary.

EXERCISE 18

—Come up with four ideas for a half-hour television documentary. Write a paragraph proposal for each. Take one of the ideas and turn it into a scene-by-scene treatment.

Writing the Mainstream Television Documentary

Normally the writer of mainstream documentaries is hired after a producer has come up with the idea for a documentary. A writer is brought in to do the research on the subject and to write a treatment and a script with the understanding that the script might well be modified in the editing stage.

For example, I have written a documentary for television on the use of animals for medical research and another documentary on a group of ophthalmologists who donated their medical skills for various periods to treating eye problems in a clinic in Haiti.

Research for the project involved learning about the history of the use of animals in medical research, the problems that have been encountered, the criticism of using animals for research, the medical discoveries that have come about specifically as a result of animal studies, and the way in which the specific research facility being concentrated on functioned.

Because of the level of information needed, a voice-over narration was decided on and was written in advance of the editing. The decision was made about what images would accompany the narration. In addition, researchers, workers, critics, and people whose lives have been saved as a result of such research were written in to be interviewed.

As documentary writer you soon learn that there are two ways to get interview subjects to say what you want them to say or approximately what you want them to say. First, you script what they will say and they memorize it or read it from a prompter. The British explored and still use this technique, but it has some definite drawbacks. Of course, there is the ethical question of whether you are implying to viewers that what they are seeing is spontaneous and unscripted. Even if this doesn't bother the writer/producer/director, the inability of most nonactors to learn to read lines convincingly or read a prompter makes this a highly problematic route to take. What will work, though it is more costly, is to record an extended discussion with the subject, perhaps injecting questions concerning the subject you wish to explore. With half an hour or more of interview on tape, it is usually easy enough in the editing room to find a minute or two in which the subject says essentially what you want said at that point in the script.

If you find this manipulative, you are certainly right. The writer/editor/producer/director is organizing the natural material to conform with a script, an idea, a direction, or a theme. Sometimes these ideas and themes may be modified by or greatly changed as a result of unexpected scenes, situations, and characters shot. Regardless of when it takes place, however, every documentary will involve this kind of manipulation because decisions must be made about what to leave in and what to leave out.

Given many hours of documentary material, two different editors might well come up with films that have not only different but opposing themes. It is naive to think that the material will simply suggest its own truth. Humans see events and make decisions about what they mean. Film and television documentaries organize reality in a way that not only makes sense but also gives a suggestion of meaning to the viewer. The task of the writer working with the producer/director is to decide what the producer/director wants and expects and, if possible, to include the writer's view of the subject.

Let's look at an example of how the same written narration can be juxtaposed with different documentary images to change the meaning. Note the difference in format. Many, perhaps most, documentary writers use the more traditional format you've already learned. I tend to use the European script format for documentary so that it is easier to see the juxtaposition of sound

and image. In fact, I use this form even if I know later that I'll
have to rewrite the script in a standard American format.

More Pampered Than Pets

Example 1: Scene 1

	Narrator
	(Voice-over)
A child with a bandaged head plays with a puppy. The child laughs. The puppy dashes around in the grass. The child trips, laughing, and the dog comes running to the child.	It has been estimated that more than four million lives have been saved as a result of research done on laboratory animals. The question is simple: Is it worth the sacrifice of the fifty million laboratory animals needed for this success?

Example 2

| A spider monkey, bandaged, sits motionless in a small cage. The camera moves closer to the monkey, and gradually the monkey notices the camera and turns its head slowly to look at the lens, which comes closer, revealing a tube protruding from the bandage. | It has been estimated that over four million lives have been saved as a result of research done on laboratory animals. The question is simple: Is it worth the sacrifice of the fifty million laboratory animals needed for this success? |

The statistics given above are examples. They do not reflect
current figures on animal research. However, the point and the
difference are quite clear. The words on the right remain the
same for both examples, but the images, both easy enough to
obtain, greatly alter the likely reaction of an audience. In Example 1 the clear suggestion is that the use of animals is certainly

worth the life of this child, assuming this child is one of those saved by such research. Even that is easy enough to ensure. It further suggests that the child's relationship to animals is natural and that the animal, in fact, exists to give pleasure, if not life, to the child. In Example 2, with the same narration, the implication is that animal research may not be worth the results, that the effects on the human-looking monkey are akin to sacrifice and torture. We don't know what has been done to that monkey and why it has been done.

The theme of the film is established by this first shot in the first scene, and the viewer knows what to expect. Each scene, each shot of the documentary can be quite real, quite spontaneous, but the writer has indicated which of these very real images should be used and how they should be coupled with voice-over narration.

The documentary writer also has the choice of suggesting the order of scenes, which scenes and shots follow each other.

It is often said that there are two sides to every story and it is the responsibility of the journalist and the documentary writer to present both sides. Experience shows that there are usually not two sides to every story. There are many more than two sides, many more than two ways of looking at an issue or problem. The wish to become objective and balanced often results either in an unconscious decision and subjectivity or in a chaotic and pointless exploration of the subject or story. It is better for a writer to make a decision on what the material means, on what he or she wants to say, and to write the documentary with a coherent, clear theme and set of goals. It is often reasonable to present alternate readings or positions in a documentary so that the viewer will be aware, particularly in a controversial subject, that alternate positions exist.

Writing the Vérité Documentary

Let's begin with a definition. Direct cinema, also known as *cinema vérité*, is a type of documentary in which one films an event as it happens, as opposed to reenacting or reconstructing an event after the fact. The conventions of this type of documentary include the use of a hand-held camera, a zoom lens, location sound, and sometimes a grainy, rough image.

Normally a subject is chosen with the assumption that it will contain enough visual material and dramatic event to make it interesting. Frederick Wiseman's documentaries on PBS are good examples. Wiseman, in such films as *High School, Basic Training,* and *Law and Order,* selects an institution—high school, the army, the police—and moves in with his cameras to record the events that take place. After shooting is finished, Wiseman and his staff edit and order the material shot to present a dramatic statement about the institution involved. The writing of vérité involves presenting the proposal more than preparing a script.

Normally the vérité documentary proposal is written by the filmmaker, possibly in conjunction with a writer. A general theme is given—the confusion of welfare offices, the vain attempt of police forces to control the growth of crime—and a series of potential scenes described. For example, a proposal to do a vérité documentary on a local police force might include the following.

Proposal: Police Force
A documentary by Stuart Kaminsky

The problems, dangers, and even tedium of a small-town police force will be explored by following (a) a pair of patrol officers, (b) the chief of police, (c) the local newspaper reporter who covers the police, (d) the officer who mans the desk and answers the phones. The film will present a microcosm of specific police problems and general social problems. Judging from an examination of three police forces of no more than ten officers in communities in northern Illinois, we can expect to find juvenile drug problems, family conflicts, breaking and entering, drunk driving, and various traffic encounters and accidents. The form of the film can be that of a single day, though we might have to shoot for several days to get the dramatic material needed.

Suggested sequence of events:

■ We begin in the main office of the police station early in the morning, perhaps even before dawn. We watch as calls come in, as the desk officer handles the calls, has coffee, talks to the man who delivers the morning paper.

■ We watch one of the patrol officers at home getting ready in the morning. We go out the door with him and watch him pick up his partner. We listen to the two of them discuss their previous day, problems, expectations, whatever they would normally do.

■ We move to the chief of police as he comes into the station, says hello, gets his coffee, and begins to field the various calls on his desk—complaints, requests to speak, etc.

■ Ideally we would have several film crews—one with the chief, one in the station, and several on patrol. If we can't afford multiple crews, we can shoot the film over the course of a week.

■ Of the calls that come in, if we have only one crew, we'll make decisions about which ones to go out on. We'll pick a day on which the chief gives a talk somewhere—local high school, women's club, Rotary Club—and film his talk and interaction with the audience.

■ In the evening, back in the station, we will watch the people we have been with—officers, desk sergeant, chief, reporter—closing up and turning the office over to the night shift.

■ We'll follow one of these people home, see him or her interact with family.

■ We'll close with a new shift about to go out on a call.

There have been many documentaries about the police,

but nothing has really dealt with the peculiarities of the small-town police department.

Normally, a budget and time schedule would also be included. A note would also be added indicating that variations or new directions might be taken if the events recorded take an unexpected dramatic turn.

In vérité, there would be no narrator, no voice-over. The coherence of the documentary would come from the decision about what should be shot and then decisions on the editing of scenes. Vérité films are often rewritten in the editing room.

Selling Your Documentary

Most documentaries on television are staff written or assigned, but many are produced by institutions, agencies, or companies that want to bring their ideas to television. Documentaries commissioned by agencies or institutions seldom make it to network schedules, but the opportunities for cable and public broadcasting in addition to use by agencies, schools, clubs, and companies is great.

A simple fact: More, far more, documentaries than works in any other genre are written and produced. The percentage that appear on television may be relatively small, but the total number produced and seen is enormous.

Documentary ideas can be submitted directly to local public broadcasting stations, but the writer should first find out who at the station makes decisions about documentaries. It's simple enough to call the station and ask. The next step is a letter to that person with a proposal. Your chances of getting an interview and the opportunity to pitch—yes, you have to pitch documentaries too—may depend on your credits.

A simple and yet complex suggestion that includes all kinds of television and screenwriting is that you take a course in film and/or video making. Not only will you get to know what the medium is capable of, but you will have the opportunity to create something of your own, possibly a short promotional example of the kind of documentary you would like to produce. Coming in with a proposal, a treatment, and a short promotional example will greatly increase your chances of support for final production. In fact, for a documentary writer even more than a writer of narrative, some training in production is essential.

An even more promising avenue for getting your documentary script produced is to find the agency, institution, or company that might be interested in your idea. Here too you need a proposal, a treatment, and a short promotional example. And here too you will have to pitch your idea.

Find the institution or institutions that might be interested in your idea and get the name of the director of public relations. Send a letter presenting your idea and the fact that you have supporting material. Hopefully, you will be called in to pitch your idea.

For example, the idea of a film on research using laboratory animals might be taken to groups as diverse as antivivisection organizations and pharmaceutical companies or hospitals engaged in animal research.

The important thing is to come up with an idea and a treatment that haven't been done before or to suggest a way of looking at the subject that may not have been considered before.

The next chapter contains more detailed advice on selling your work and examines, among other things, television markets.

PART
THREE

THE BUSINESS OF WRITING FOR TELEVISION

The next three chapters contain information on the business aspect of television:

- How to protect your script, how to obtain an agent, and how to explore the television market.
- Detailed information on the decision makers in the industry, on how the production process operates, on networks, and on the roles of both the producer and the director in television.
- Information on breaking into the industry.

11

PROTECTING YOUR SCRIPT, FINDING A MARKET AND AN AGENT

Protecting Your Script and Ideas

Aspiring television writers too often develop a near paranoia about protecting their ideas, treatments, and scripts. This desire for protection comes from a fear that your idea or script will be so good that an unscrupulous producer will be unable to resist the urge to steal your creation. That does, indeed, happen, but it is so rare that it is not worth much consideration. The reason is simple. Producers are looking for talented writers. If you are talented, it is your ongoing talent they will want, not a single idea or script. Taken from another perspective, it is relatively inexpensive to purchase your script or idea. A major producer will simply pay you rather than run the risk of complaint and challenge. Reputations are a major currency of television producers. Numerous complaints by writers can undermine that reputation.

Garner Simmons:

"If it's a great idea, maybe this producer reads it and gets turned on by it and decides, 'Hell, why do I need this kid to tag along? I'll just steal the idea and do it myself.' In reality, while it happens occasionally, I'm sure, I think you just have to understand that the town doesn't work that way."

It is true, however, that readers, producers, actors, and directors sometimes reject a script or an idea and later find it creeping unconsciously into their development of a made-for-television film or a series episode. That inadvertent borrowing is fairly common and is something you should protect yourself against.

There are two ways to protect your scripts. The copyright information that follows is presented as a guideline. For specific advice, *please consult your attorney*.

1. You can obtain a copyright from the Library of Congress. To do this, write to Register of Copyrights, Library of Congress, Washington, DC 29559 and request an Application for Copyright Registration for a Work of the Performing Arts. The completed three-page form must be filled out, signed, and returned to the copyright office with a $10 check or money order. Both published and unpublished works can be registered.

According to the copyright office, you can copyright works "prepared for the purpose of being 'performed' directly before an audience or indirectly 'by means of any device or process.' " Works of performing arts include musical works including accompanying words, dramatic works including any accompanying music, pantomimes and choreographic works, and "motion pictures and other audiovisual works."

You will need to deposit with your application one complete copy of every unpublished work, two complete copies of any published work, and one complete copy of the first foreign edition of your work.

Your basic copyright for works you have created is for the life of the author plus fifty years. For works made for hire—including scripts—the duration of the copyright is seventy-five years from publication or a hundred years from creation, whichever is shorter.

There are some things you cannot copyright or protect. You cannot copyright a title. You may be in trouble if someone takes you to court claiming that you purposely called your telefilm *On the Waterfront* in the hope that viewers would identify it with the original film. However, if you have a film appropriately titled *On the Waterfront*, you have a perfect right to use that title. Conversely, if you create a title and copyright your series or film, someone else might use that same title with impunity unless the script of that film or television show and yours are so similar that copyright infringement is evident. I have twice run into this problem. I was working on a novel titled *High Midnight* about a highly fictionalized Gary Cooper. I discovered that a made-for-television film existed with that title. The made-for-television movie had nothing to do with my book and nothing to do with the movie *High Noon*. Two months before my novel *Red Chameleon* was published another novel with that title was released. Like mine, the other novel dealt with the Soviet Union. However, it was quite evident that the two books were very different and that it probably wasn't to the advantage of either to have the same title. Both of my books went to press with the titles noted above.

2. A second way to protect your television writing is to register your script with the Writers Guild Registration Service. You can obtain information and forms for doing this by writing to Writers Guild of America, West, Inc., 8955 Beverly Blvd., Los Angeles, CA 90048. The cost for registering your script with the WGA is $5 for members and $10 for nonmembers.

The guild's registration service was established to help television and film writers establish the completion date and identity of their literary property written for movies, television, and radio. According to the WGA, "a writer has certain rights under the law the moment the work is completed. It is therefore important that the date of completion be legally established."

Registration with the WGA does not provide legal protection, nor does the WGA registration office compare registration deposits to determine similarity among works or give legal opinions or advice, but it does provide evidence of the writer's claim to authorship of the material and the date of its completion.

You can register the following with the WGA: formats, outlines, synopses, story lines, or scripts for movies, television, or radio. The WGA does not accept book manuscripts, plays, music, lyrics illustrations, or articles of public record. Every property must be registered separately, with one exception: Three episodes, sketches, or skits written for an existing television or radio series may be deposited as a single registration.

Material deposited with the WGA is registered for a five-year term. At the end of five years you can renew for an additional five years. Renewal is $5 for members, $10 for nonmembers. If you don't renew, the guild destroys the material without notice.

For obvious reasons, the registered copy on deposit should not normally be returned to the writer. Once it leaves the WGA you no longer have evidence of its deposit date. There are, however, instances in which you might want or need the work returned. To do so, you must give forty-eight hours' notice to the WGA and submit the proper signed documents.

Finding a Television Market

Once again, the Writers Guild of America is invaluable. When you write to the guild, you should also request information on obtaining membership. Membership in the WGA requires accumulating twelve credits for stories, scripts, rewrites, and polishes. It's fairly complicated, and information should be obtained from the WGA.

However, it is possible to obtain copies of the WGA *Newsletter*. The *Newsletter* periodically publishes a television market list indicating the series that are in production, the production company, and the contact person for the series. The listing also indicates whether all scripts are committed for the current season, whether the series accepts submissions through agents only, and the genre of particular series—episodic drama, episodic comedy, anthology, serial, comedy/variety, dramatic comedy, romantic comedy, variety, or action adventure.

There are currently thirty separate production companies creating scripts for more than eighty-five series for network, cable, and syndication. These companies range from Paramount and Universal, which currently have nine or ten series in production, to companies such as Alien Productions, which is producing a single series (*ALF*).

Other Markets

There are several additional markets that are often overlooked by writers but that can not only be lucrative but can lead to contacts, credits, and the possibility of working in other television formats.

CHILDREN'S PROGRAMS

The children's market, particularly Saturday morning and weekday afternoon animated series, is an interesting and specialized market. Many of these series are done in segments of eight- to nine-minute episodes. Some are in half-hour units. Since the series are animated, they have none of the considerations of scope that are essential in live-action television. For example, it costs no more to send your animated characters to a castle than to place them in an apartment. Before writing for animated series, as with other series, you should study the genre, watch the episodes to see the kinds of stories and characters being presented. The illusion of realism in dialogue is not a consideration in this genre. Neither are many of the other factors we have gone over, but story and character are still essential.

When you've studied the genre or particular series you are interested in, find out what company produces the series and get the name of the series' producer from the credits. Then write an individual episode and either send it directly to the producer with a covering letter indicating that you would be interested in writing for that series or another series that company might be producing or send a letter to the producer with your résumé and a statement indicating that you have a script and, possibly, a list of ideas for additional stories.

Scripts for animated series are the same as scripts for live-action shows.

GAME SHOWS AND QUIZ SHOWS

Many of these shows require people who write gags for the hosts and questions for the contestants to answer. As with animated shows, study the show and then contact the producer with a sample page of gags and another page of questions.

TALK SHOWS, VARIETY SHOWS, SPECIALS

This is a harder market to break and a very specialized one. As with the others, study the host and listen to the instructions. Instead of writing a series of gags, prepare a brief, timely opening monologue. Before you do so, time the opening monologue of the show to which you are submitting material. It's a good idea to start with a local show rather than shooting for Johnny Carson or David Letterman. For one thing, it will give you experience. For another, it will give you credits. This is another genre in which local cable can be helpful in developing your talents. Your best chance on the national level is to find a comic, preferably a regular guest on a talk show, who is willing to read submissions of jokes from outside writers. Many comedians of this sort get a great deal of material this way.

What an Agent Does

Simply stated, an agent works for you. He or she takes your material and tries to sell it. If successful, he or she also takes a cut of the money for the sale, traditionally ten percent.

Harlan Ellison:

"Without an agent you are really leaving yourself wide open for trouble. That is, unless you *enjoy* being mugged."

Larry Gelbart:

"An agent has access to production companies that are not open to free-lance talent. If you can, you should try to get your material to an agent as the first step in becoming known for the kind of work you do."

Garner Simmons:

"Once you have an agent, he or she in theory goes to work for you, beginning to open those doors you can't open yourself. However, it does another thing. It also offers you a kind of credibility. Having an agent says to any producer in town, 'Here's somebody who is seriously pursuing his or her craft and has the credibility of having gotten somebody else interested in the work.' "

Production executives like agents because lawsuits only very, very rarely arise over the originality of material submitted to them by accredited agencies.

Harlan Ellison:

"With all the lawsuits from idiots who think they've been plagiarized, studios are very, very leery and will not go near an unsolicited manuscript. They have good cause."

Garner Simmons:

"It protects the producer from lawsuits because if it comes from an agency there is a kind of unwritten law that says 'Listen, we're not trying to rip anybody off, but at the same time we don't want to be sued because there are any number of cases in town in which there were similar ideas on the table.' Producers try to avoid at all costs any additional legal matters."

Obtaining an Agent

How can you get someone in a position to help you to look at your material?

Larry Gelbart:

"Some people chant mantras, other people light candles. It's pretty rare that someone can present a piece of material to the most obvious target, that is to say the producer of a successful show or the star of a successful series. Most often you need a representative, an agent."

Garner Simmons:

"The key element in getting into a career as a professional writer in the entertainment industry is somehow finding an agent. An agent is a very important cog in this whole process. Agents are more and more in control of the business because they are taking over those positions within the studios and within the networks that buy material. So, you have agents pitching to ex-agents.

"You must realize that agents are on both sides of the table today. Without them your work doesn't ever make it into view of anybody who can get it made. You basically just have to accept that that is the most important path you have when you come out to the West Coast and break into the business. Finding an agent is as critical a thing as anything you can do. It is pivotal in writing the best scripts you can write to attract that agent."

The WGA publishes an agency list that can be obtained from Writers Guild of America, West., Inc., 8955 Beverly Blvd., Los Angeles, CA 90048. The list changes every three months or so. To get a copy, send a note requesting one and include a check or money order for $1 to cover postage and handling.

Before submitting material to an agency on the WGA list, write to the individual agency indicating your professional and/or academic credentials and describe the material you would like to submit. The agency will respond, letting you know if you should send the material for its consideration.

Most agencies will return material sent to them if you include a self-addressed, stamped envelope. However, individual agencies are under no obligation to return any material submitted for consideration.

Agents are the Catch-22 of the industry. You need them to get an audience, a hearing, but you usually can't get an agent until you have some credits or are referred by a working writer, usually a client of that agent.

Larry Gelbart:

"Most people run into the old bugaboo about 'We won't take anybody on until you get some experience.' And, 'Well, how can I get any experience unless you take me on?' "

Bob Shayne:

"There are two parts to becoming a writer. One is to write things, and the other is to get people to read them."

Many agencies simply are not taking on new writers, and they make this evident. Other agencies, the larger ones, often serve as packaging agencies, which means they put together projects—script, actor, director—before they approach a producer or a network. Therefore, they are unlikely to take on a new writer.

There are, however, agents who are willing to look at the work of new writers. There are more than a hundred agencies representing television and film writers. In their listings the agencies indicate whether they are willing to look at unsolicited material. There are even agents and independent producers who are actively looking for new writers to represent and work with. The reasons are varied, but an important one is that new writers are less expensive than established guild writers. This works both to your advantage and to your disadvantage. You may get a hearing, a pitch, a reading because you have no credits or few of them and you hold the promise or possibility of talented, inexpensive writing. The disadvantage, obviously, is that you will be paid relatively little for your initial efforts.

Garner Simmons:

"You will notice that the list runs a couple of hundred agents and that some of them have an asterisk next to them. That asterisk indicates that those agents are interested in looking at the work of novice writers. They are obviously not nearly as many. Maybe one-tenth of the agents on the list have an asterisk next to their name."

Such agencies are the best bet for a beginning writer with no connections. Remember, however, write to them first.

Other agencies will accept unsolicited material only from

writers who have been referred to them by one of their clients or someone known to that agency—a writer, producer, director, etc. So, as I indicated earlier in this book, it is a good idea to attend seminars, workshops, and classes taught by professional television writers who can assess your work and, if they like it, recommend an agency.

Some media professionals are not entirely sold on the advantages of agents to beginning writers.

Garry Marshall:

"It's my subjective opinion that an agent is not very good at getting your first job. I think you always have to get your first job yourself, and then the agent will get you a better deal and get you more work once you have credits."

I had two disastrous encounters with agents, one of whom was incompetent and the other of whom served me tea when I came to New York and thought it was improper to be aggressive in selling an author's work. My third and present agent has been and continues to be knowledgeable, aggressive, and extremely successful.

I supply the work. He supplies the criticism, knows the market, and sells the product. The product includes professionally written spec scripts, treatments, proposals, and scripts.

Not every agent will break his or her back to sell your writing. When and if you pursue the agency route, you can do a great many things to take an active role in the whole process of getting your work sold.

Garner Simmons:

"Don't submit your work to one agent and if that agent turns you down turn around and give it to another one. That will take you forever. Submit it to all of them and see what happens. That means making multiple copies, which is a little more expensive, but you are going to get an answer a lot faster. And some of them, hopefully, will be interested."

Bob Shayne:

"You can't leave your destiny up to strangers. They will disappoint you. You must take it into your own hands. Even if, first of all, you get an agent, you must make sure that the agent that you sign with is a reputable agent, *more* than a reputable agent—someone in the center of big-time show business. About the only way you can do it is by asking the agents to give you a list of their clients. They probably won't give you a list, but they'll probably name some. If they can name three or four very, very major, hot clients, you know it's possible that this is an agency that really functions. You are worse off with a small-time agent than with no agent.

"Secondly, even after you get this big agent, you must not rely on this big agent to do the selling for you. He's not going to do it. For the most part, you're still going to have to do it for yourself. After you get the big agent, or if you can't get the big agent, either way, you must then devote half of your time to selling yourself."

Once again, I would suggest that when you approach an agency you do so with more than one example of your work. Agencies differ on what they want to see, but I would advise that you provide at least a one-hour dramatic script and a half-hour comedy or two dramatic scripts and two comedies. If you can show your versatility with the two scripts, that is even better. If you have a made-for-television script, submit that too. Your dramatic and comedy scripts can either be spec scripts for existing series or a combination of spec scripts and originals. If you have to err either way, submit more specs than originals. The made-for-television script will demonstrate your ability to create original works, but your specs will probably give you a slightly better chance at getting your work read, or at least glanced at.

CHAPTER
12

WHO MAKES THE DECISIONS?

Producers, Networks, and Decisions

While there are dozens of ways of getting a story or series idea to television, a few avenues are most common.

Individual production companies with established records initiate ideas and possibly even develop them to the script stage and propose a package (a salable entity including such things as potential actors or stars, a completed script, and even a proposed budget). The established record of Lorimar, Aaron Spelling, Stephen Cannell, MTM, and Garry Marshall, for example, gives them access to the networks, including cable. The vast majority of individual shows—made-for-television movies, series, specials—that appear on television are proposed by producers or production companies. The individuals who run these companies, who serve as the creative forces within them, began by working for others in similar positions. Stephen Cannell, for example, began by working for Roy Huggins, who produced such shows as *Maverick* and *The Rockford Files*.

Once a writer is established, often by doing dozens of scripts for an established producer, the writer can propose his or her own ideas for a series or show to the producer or directly to the networks or cable networks. Normally, such proposals are made through the writer's agent.

Is television, then, a producer's medium?

Jeff Rice:

"Producers on TV have tremendous clout and in general are the authority figures."

Bob Shayne:

"In television, producers tend to be the boss. It is true in television that a project is generally started by a writer and/or a producer. And it is developed with the money coming from a network, some development money coming from a production company, perhaps, and then the major amount, the script money, coming from a network. During this whole process, the producer has been in charge . . . I have become a producer strictly to protect myself as a writer."

Garner Simmons:

"Television is the producer's medium, and as a writer in television, what you begin to realize, provided you have the ability and to some degree the background and the patience for it, is that you need to protect your own writing. And the way you do that is to become a producer. If you can push at it long and hard enough, you can get to the point where nobody rewrites you. That's an ideal situation."

Bill Nuss:

"Writers move up the ladder from free-lance to term writer to story editor to executive story editor to producer to supervising producer to executive producer. They are basically made producers to have more control over their work."

Larry Gelbart:

"A beginning writer's got to demonstrate his ability as a writer. You can't walk before you make other people crawl. You have to demonstrate your expertise. With success you're going to be given more and more responsibility. And you can't be given more responsibility as a writer than to become responsible for other people's scripts as well."

Garry Marshall:

"The traditional cliché is that in theater the writer is king, in television the producer is king, and in movies the director is king. That's pretty much accurate. In television the producer is boss. I used to give an open speech to every writer who joined the staff of my shows, saying they probably have a lot of ideas they want to do but it is not their turn yet. It's the producer's turn; eventually the writers will get their turn. Television writers executes someone's vision until they are producers."

A writer cannot become a producer or make series proposals until he or she has sufficient knowledge of the industry—the trends, genres, economics—to make a reasonable presentation.

Very few ideas, even those from major producers, make their way to the development stage—the stage at which money is put up by the production company and possibly the network to prepare a finished script or scripts and a proposed budget. Of those that are put into development, only a few—perhaps thirty to fifty a year—are financed for a pilot. A pilot is a single episode made to be shown to the network executives to convince them to accept the show as a potential series. Most pilots are half-hour episodes for comedy series (or game shows, specials, etc.). One-hour dramatic series proposals are usually funded as movies-of-the-week or possibly even miniseries. A movie-of-the-week is normally more cost-efficient because it can be sold independently to a network even if a decision is later made not to produce a series. Movies-of-the-week also have the advantage of reshowings or possibly videotape or foreign sales. Half-hour pilots seldom reach the public, with the rare exception of summer fill-ins.

Producers become producers for several reasons. One, obviously, is that they want to make money. More important, however, is that they want their ideas, their projects produced. Series stars—Mary Tyler Moore, Elizabeth Montgomery, Ron Howard, Desi Arnaz, and Lucille Ball, for example—may also have enough power/contact/clout to use their success to become producers.

The point to remember here is that in all likelihood you must pay your dues, learn to work on the scripts of others, before you get the chance to develop your own ideas.

Bob Shayne:

"That is basically the answer to getting any kind of writing; you must, absolutely must, do your homework and pay your dues and all of those clichés. And put in the time and effort and have the talent, the ideas."

The Production Process

Understanding how and how many shows are produced should give you a good idea of the odds a beginning writer faces. Of the few pilots made, an even smaller number actually make it to the series stage—perhaps a dozen (about nine percent of those made) a year on the commercial networks, another dozen on cable. It is true that the number of markets has increased through the recent expansion of Fox Television and the interest of cable networks—HBO, Showtime, Cinemax, and USA among others—in entering into series production. Still, the number of new shows is small, perhaps two dozen a year. Of that two dozen, only a handful, perhaps half, are successful enough to complete a full season. Further, a show has to run four to five complete seasons (at least a hundred shows) in order for syndication—and big money—to become possible.

Once the decision is made to make a show or a series, even before it goes into production, revisions are made in the proposal and script. The revisions, often not done by the original writer, are necessitated by many factors. A network may alter the original concept to suit its scheduling needs, the form of the show may have to be altered for budgetary reasons, or an actor for whom the concept must be altered may be cast.

Normally when a show becomes a series, a writing team works on it from week to week, episode to episode. The story line for the series is worked out, developed by the show's producer, story editor, and staff. Many, if not most, of the scripts for the series are written by the regular staff. However, quite a few of the episodes are written by free-lance writers. The free-lance writers, including new writers, are selected on the basis of their past work and on the basis of spec scripts submitted through an agent, to the production company, or directly to the network. Writers are suggested by other writers, and it is common for the producer of one series to send a free-lance writer who has produced a spec script to another producer who appears to be a more appropriate potential employer of the writer. A spec script may be submitted to *Hunter*, for example, and one of the staff writers on *Hunter* may believe the writer of the script is more appropriate for *Dynasty*.

Pitching

There is another skill that television writers need, particularly writers of comedy—the ability to pitch. Pitching is a fact of the industry, and it simply means orally presenting your ideas in condensed form. The writer who has drawn the interest of a producer through a spec script or referral will often be called in to present a proposal for an episode. By the same token, the producer of a potential series will usually begin by making a pitch to a network executive or executives. A writer called in to make a pitch will normally address the series' producer or the story editor.

Harlan Ellison:

"Pitching is more important than anything else. The one thing producers look for in a writer is not talent; it is dependability. Dependability takes many forms. Dependability for them begins with the way you present yourself when you come in.

"What they expect is a kind of confidence, an ability to speak on your feet, an ability to think on your feet. A pitch session is a session in which you must establish that you know what you are doing. It's like being a stand-up comic, working to a hostile crowd. Watch their faces. You've got to know body language. Get a copy of the book *Body Language.* Also, read Conan Doyle's Sherlock Holmes series to learn deductive logic. Body language and deductive language will tell you everything you need to know to give a proper pitch. Convince them you know what you're doing, be confident, and they'll breathe a sigh of relief."

Larry Gelbart:

"[*The pitch is the writer's*] one chance really to sell an idea, so it's important. I wouldn't rehearse pitching. Some people make a pitch that is almost a stand-up routine. And some people pitch much better than they finally execute. Pitching is selling, and what really sells a script eventually is on the page, not in the conference. I know some people on the other side of the desk, the executive side, who get very caught up with how a person is performing in a pitch, and that is, in a way, very unfair. I wouldn't trust a writer who wasn't nervous and anxious about what he was pitching. It's a stressful situation. You have to be honest with yourself. It's okay to feel hot under the collar, to be tense. I think the really good staff people on the receiving end of the pitch ought to do all they can to make the pitcher comfortable.

"When you pitch, know your subject, know it well. Try to anticipate probing questions. You can sometimes be caught off guard in a very constructive way. Someone may ask you something that hadn't occurred to you, and that might help your idea. It's just important to go in feeling that you know your idea very well."

Bill Nuss:

"It's very important. It's something I really wasn't taught in school. People have short attention spans, and you have to be able to sell something before they lose it. You come into someone's office and they say 'Entertain me!'

"Somebody's got to come in and say 'Hey! Here's a story you haven't thought about doing or maybe you have and haven't done yet.' This person has to tell us in five or ten minutes a terrific little story with a beginning, a middle, and an end. They don't have to have all the little details and all the beef. We don't want to hear about that. We just want to hear a beginning, a good hook, what the middle is, and how it ends. Also, we want to know what happens with our characters.

"Some people are good at it, some people are bad at it. It can be a problem. There are some very, very funny comedy writers who aren't funny in the room. There are others that are hysterical in the room. Same with drama. It's sort of a developed skill. You learn how to play a room. If you get a chance to pitch, be brief, think, entertain. Hit the beats that will sell the story. Don't go on too long, especially if it's working."

Garry Marshall:

"Pitching in comedy is critical because if you can make the person you're pitching to laugh, they figure you might be a good writer. In dramas, it really doesn't matter. It's all in the story. I think pitching is one of the tools of the comedy writer. The writer should pitch concisely. Do what they do in football. Watch the quarterback's eyes. As soon as he starts to wander, you've got to pitch a little faster. Other than that, don't pitch too long. I am an advocate of rehearsing your pitch in front of people before you go in to pitch. It's no good to pitch into a tape recorder because traditionally writers don't like the sound of their own voice. You don't have to know how it sounds, just that you're keeping the other person interested."

Jeff Rice:

"Pitching saves the producer from having to read anything right up to (sometimes including) the point where the purchased product has been reworked by old-line pros into its final, shooting script form. Don't be cocky or excitable but come in clothed in confidence and enthusiasm. Make your pitch, thank the producer for his time, and get out. If a producer suggests changes that you know will destroy your story, tell him he's a genius and suggest he contact your agent immediately to set up a contract. Then, when you've got it and your advance money, destroy your story to suit the producer's ideas. As W. C. Fields so succinctly put it: 'Find out what they got. Git it. Git.' ''

Bob Shayne:

''Pitching a story, unfortunately, is more important than writing a story. You don't get paid for writing a story until you have pitched it and impressed the person you pitched it to so much that they hire you. Or, more likely, they recommend you to people over them, and they get several people to agree to hire you to go ahead and write it. I find this unfortunate. But don't slough off the process of pitching. It is more important than how well you write. I would take at least one day, preferably two whole days, to prepare for that meeting. This is after you have the ideas and you have them as worked out as you want them. Rehearse however it works best for you. Have a friend pretend to be the buyer or do it in front of a mirror or do it in your car, but do it and do it several times. The day that you are going to meet, have nothing on your agenda but this meeting, nothing to split your concentration. Take the pitching process at least as seriously as the writing. Frankly, it is more important.''

Garner Simmons:

''Pitching is critical. . . . I've seen terrible stories, stories that could not be done, sold because they were told so well they couldn't be turned down. . . . Walk in with a grabber, something they don't expect. Then use the next few lines to fill in the grabber. If they are really interested, you'll have them hooked, and you can reel them in by telling them the story and having all the answers they need. [Screenwriter and director] Paul Schrader has suggested that you pitch a movie, any movie, with a grabber of an opening, three absolutely smashing scenes that rivet the listener to his seat, and an unbelievable finale.

''You should always go in with at least three stories to pitch, because the first one may fall squarely on its nose or they may already have something like it. If you pitch three good stories, even if they don't buy them, you are more likely to be brought back to pitch again. Make it seem that you have a limitless supply of stories and that you really understand how their stories work and who their characters are.

"You will be faced with two, three, or four people, probably a supervising producer, who is sort of the head writer on the series, perhaps another writer/producer, and a staff writer or two. They will be listening for something that really sparkles. Nine out of ten times the people who buy your material are going on gut feelings and hunches. You need talent, persistence, and luck. For example, if you go in and pitch something that is a great story but doesn't really fit their series, don't expect the person you are pitching to to pick up the phone and call the guy in charge of two-hour movies to tell him to suggest that you pitch to him."

If you are called in to make a pitch for a specific series based on a sample or spec script, you should have at least six ideas for episodes in that series. You should also be prepared to pitch each one for two to five minutes.

The pitch for a made-for-television film or a new series can be anything from ten minutes or less to half an hour. It is seldom more and it is seldom that long. The idea of the pitch is to convince the producer or network exec that your story, your proposal, your series is exciting, original, and has a potentially significant audience.

Note that I said "potentially significant." That usually means a broad audience, a large audience, but that is not always the case. Networks and producers are, with increasing frequency, willing to try the significant, the unusual, even if it does not promise a mass audience initially.

To be successful at the pitch you must be able to perform, to think on your feet. Many writers, even successful writers, are simply unable to do this. Some of them team up with others who are more outgoing as partners. Some succeed in spite of their difficulty. In the pitch the prepared writer does not start by telling the story but by giving the highlights of the idea, the things that make this story different, worth doing. The writer who begins by giving plot may not be given enough time to present those highlights.

An important note: Never, never do any writing for nothing. Sit down, talk to a producer, to anyone who is interested in your talents, but put nothing on paper—other than spec scripts—without at least token payment. The temptation is great to do otherwise, but you lose by doing so. You lose the respect of the person you are trying most to impress, and you let yourself in for doing a great deal of unrewarded work. If it doesn't cost the producer anything to get work out of you, the amount you are asked to do may as well increase because it will cost the same—nothing.

As a beginning writer, your first pitch is likely to be to a producer or to a story editor. Essentially, you must present your idea for the script you want to write for that series as directly and dramatically as possible. You are not simply telling a story. You are selling a story. There's a difference. You may not even be given enough time to tell a story. The writer who presents a good pitch has indicated to the producer or story editor how that idea could come to life, could be produced. Some people are naturals at it. Others have to learn. And some of it *can* be learned.

One of my favorite pitch stories appears in Budd Schulberg's novel *The Disenchanted*. Schulberg, who made many a pitch himself, created a character based on F. Scott Fitzgerald. In the novel the Fitzgerald character, who is a staff writer for a movie studio, is called in before studio executives and told to pitch a movie. The character has no idea of what he will say. All he has is a title, *Winter Carnival*. Added to this is the fact that the character is hung over from the night before. The Fitzgerald character proceeds to improvise a tale with no idea of where it is going. He watches the sour faces of the old men around him, sweats in agony and certainty that he will be stopped and thrown out, and plunges on, sometimes actually losing himself in the tale. When he is finished, the studio executive readily accepts the idea and tells the writer to get to work on it. The

Fitzgerald character wanders out wondering if he can remember any of the story and details he has just pitched.

In fact, the Schulberg story was based on a real incident and a real film, *Winter Carnival,* which was made by Columbia Pictures.

SUGGESTIONS FOR SUCCESSFUL PITCHING

The following twenty points are not rules—there *are* no rules for pitching. They're merely suggestions that might help you face this necessary ordeal.

1. If you've been told that you will have fifteen minutes, assume you'll have only five or six. Don't save your best ideas for the end. You may never be given a chance to get to them.

2. Don't start at the beginning. Don't tell the story. Begin by indicating what is unique about your episode or idea. Compare it to other series or episodes in the same series if necessary. Be prepared to summarize your story or idea in a sentence or two. Think in terms of an ad or, as many suggest, an entry in your local television guide. So, on a card or sheet, you might write:

Carol watched her husband murdered in a drive-in parking lot and almost lost her sanity. Fighting her way back to sanity, she devotes herself to her two children and to physical fitness. She opens a highly successful workout center and is about to sign a contract for a television series when she finds that the men who murdered her husband are back . . . and looking for her.

3. If you've got a particularly good idea for a scene or an exchange of dialogue, give it.

4. When you do tell the story, if you get that far, keep it brief—highlights only. Don't get into details unless the detail is a highlight, a joke, or a gimmick that you think might help sell your story.

5. Be flexible. A lot of what you will do will require improvisation. Come prepared with variations on your idea. The thought and directions you discarded when you worked up your pitch should be available for instant use.

Example: Along with a producer I recently pitched a made-for-television mystery idea to CBS. One of our major gimmicks was the idea of referring to television detectives of the past by having characters in our film reminiscent of TV detectives the viewer might be familiar with. One of the people at CBS pointed out that the idea had been done before. We immediately pointed out that it was but one of the many ideas we had, and while we still thought it could work because it was quite different from what had been done before, we were not only able to go to another idea—fictional detectives in film or print—but also to discard that element completely without losing the essence of our film. We were pitching. They were catching. If they didn't like what we pitched, it was our job to throw something different that they might like.

6. Be prepared to suggest actors for any roles you create, though you might never be asked.

7. Prepare a one-page, two pages at most, written pitch you can leave with the person or persons to whom you are pitching. Begin with the highlights, keep the story minimal, and be brief.

Here's an example of a proposal I prepared for such a pitch. The film, with a number of changes, was written by me and produced by Empire Pictures:

Proposal: ENEMY TERRITORY
The tale begins late in the evening. Bill Carey, a white telephone repairman, enters one of the buildings in a low-income high-rise development in the inner city to check on reports of telephone malfunction, a frequent problem in the development. It is his last stop of the day before he heads home, where he lives alone. He is uncomfortable, a bit surly about having to enter the building, which is inhabited exclusively by black tenants. On the way in, Carey accidentally jostles a ten-year-old boy. The boy shouts abuse at Carey, who threatens to spank the kid. Carey then goes up to the nineteenth-floor apartment to check the phones. He

discovers that all the phones in the building are out and he cannot repair them on his own.

In the hall on his way out, Carey encounters a group of boys, one of them the kid he jostled in the lobby. A knife is pulled and a bigger boy advances on Carey, saying the gang is going to take him apart. Carey, outnumbered and fully aware of the danger he faces, is saved by a well-dressed black man, Bill Knott, who is in the building to deliver an insurance policy. The kids, seeing the odds change, back off but vow to be back before the two men can get out of the building.

Carey and Knott head for the elevator but find it isn't working. It could be the normal state of disrepair in the building or a purposeful act by the gang. The two men hear the freight elevator coming up and move toward it. Before the elevator reaches their level they see that it is filled with armed boys, including a group that confronted them. Carey and Knott scramble for the stairway door.

From this point on, the tale becomes one in which the two men must work their way down to the main floor before the gang gets to them.

Among their adventures on the way are:

- an encounter with an old couple. The woman wants to help the two men. The old man wants to turn them in to the gang.
- an encounter with a young, cynical, well-educated woman who, in spite of herself, helps them and is attracted to Knott.
- an encounter with a little girl who serves as guide to the two men and knows places for them to hide.
- at least two confrontations with members of the gang and a fight on an outdoor seventh-floor landing in which one of the gang members gets killed.

Carey and Knott eventually make it out of the building with the help of sympathetic residents and their own resources. It will take them all night, and just when it appears that they have made it to safety they will be confronted by the gang. Carey will be wounded, seriously but not fatally, and Knott will have to face the gang leader in a one-on-one battle. Knott defeats the leader, and just as the gang advances on the two men the police arrive, scattering the gang.

The film ends with Carey on a stretcher, reaching out to grasp Knott's hand in thanks.

8. Have a title ready, one that will remind the person to whom you are pitching of your particular story or episode. In the example of the movie-of-the week pitch, our working title was *Murder in Disguise*. If you think the title is strong, use it in making your pitch. Don't just say "my story" or "our project." Say "In *Murder in Disguise* . . ."

9. Be businesslike and don't push. As the sign says in Mel Brooks's (a great pitcher) film *The Twelve Chairs,* "State your business and leave."

10. Don't read from written material. You can bring a few notes, but don't read. I know there are people who do it successfully, but I don't recommend it. Come prepared, if you like, with a passage or a scene to read, but don't read it unless you are asked to.

11. Rehearse what you are going to say, at least the core of your presentation. Time it and keep the part you memorize brief.

12. Don't hold back. Of course you always run the risk of your ideas being taken, intentionally or unintentionally, but that isn't very likely. Again, the reason is simple. If you are a beginning writer, it is probably easier to pay you for any great ideas you have than to take them from you and run the risk of complaint.

13. Be enthusiastic and interested in your own ideas. Remember, you are probably pitching to people who hear dozens of pitches a month. If you aren't truly interested in what you

are presenting, you can't expect a producer or a story editor to be interested. What interests you about your idea? Tell them. This doesn't mean that you shouldn't be yourself. Convey enthusiasm the way you usually do, according to your own personality.

14. If at all possible, find out something about the person or persons to whom you are pitching. What have they done before? What are their credits? If you truly like something they have done, it might be reasonable to indicate that when the pitch is over, if the opportunity arises.

15. Rehearse, preferably to a person whose judgment you trust. Tape your basic pitch if you are comfortable with the sound of your own voice. It may be awkward for you, but it will give you a good sense of how you sound to others.

16. Watch the face or faces of the people you are pitching to. Look at them when you pitch and listen to them when they ask a question. Clarify or go on to another point if the person you are pitching to looks bored or distracted.

17. Be prepared to go with an idea the person you are pitching to picks up on. If he or she likes a particular character or idea you didn't plan to emphasize, explore the character or idea. Listen, listen, listen. Consider the possibility of making the character or the idea more central. The important thing in the pitch is to sell yourself. You must be flexible. Later, perhaps, if you are hired for the project, you may suggest that you go back to your original idea. More often, however, the person you are pitching to will come up with something quite reasonable that you would do well to pick up on.

18. Be yourself and do your best to relax. Don't tighten up.

19. Dress as if you take the pitch seriously. Being laid back may be a reasonable life-style, but it's a style many producers and working writers feel you should earn. It doesn't matter how

casually the person you are pitching to dresses; you should come dressed as if you mean business. Some people dress casually and act casual at pitches because they fear being rejected and want to create the impression that the meeting isn't all that important to them. Well, it is important. They know it and you know it. It is a sign of your own confidence that you respect the importance of that meeting.

20. When you hear "thank you" from the person you are pitching to, shake hands, tell him or her that you are pleased to have been given the chance to make the pitch, and get out. Don't ask when you will hear from them. Don't continue to try to sell your idea.

When you do get the opportunity to pitch, learn from it. If you don't succeed in selling your idea, try to figure out what you did wrong, if anything. If you're lucky, you'll get some feedback from the people you pitched to, but don't count on it. Consider each pitch a learning experience and look forward to the next.

Some people love pitching. I do. Others hate it but overcome their hatred and fear and learn to do it.

All right. The pitch is done. The writer has been convincing. The spec is applauded or at least given some credit for professionalism. The next step, normally, is for the writer to be assigned a script to do. This means that the spec script or scripts you have written will probably never be produced. They weren't written to be produced. They were written to show your ability, your talent, your knowledge of series television, of the needs of the medium. You may be lucky and have that spec script accepted, or you may be able to adapt that spec to a series or special you eventually work on, but then again, you may not. Writing for television means writing and moving on. There is no time to fall in love with what you have written, to stop and devote days, weeks, months, years to trying to sell a single script or idea. The would-be writer, even the working professional, needs three, five, ten projects on the line. The television writer has to be able to work quickly from his own ideas and the ideas of others. A novelist can be a success in his or her career with half a dozen novels. A film writer can make a career on a dozen or eighteen features. A television writer must turn out hundreds of hours of scripts. Television is all-consuming, and those who succeed are those who can produce for it and run back to the typewriter or computer and get started again.

A caveat: While it is not only possible to write novels anywhere in the United States and get them published and it is even possible to write feature films anywhere in the United States, it is almost impossible to write for series television on a regular basis unless you live in California near the networks, near the producers, near the studios. The reason is simple. You are constantly pitching ideas, working on revisions, meeting, adapting, revising. It is the kind of work that cannot be done easily by long distance. Normally, it is easier for a producer to get another writer rather than deal with one who lives in Chicago, Dubuque, or Atlanta. Los Angeles is a land heavily populated with writers anxious to work.

That doesn't mean you should quit your job, pack your bags, and head for California. It means that you should clearly understand that if you meet some initial success and decide to pursue television writing as a career you will have to seriously consider a move. True, a considerate amount of production work is being done in other cities, particularly New York or, in Canada, Toronto and Vancouver, but the ongoing center of production for television is Los Angeles.

Working on Assignments

Now the truly hard work begins. You are given a story line and a deadline for producing it. It is not uncommon for a writer to be asked to produce a one-hour script in two or three days. It is not uncommon for a writer to be asked to rewrite a script a day or two before it is scheduled to be shot. It is not uncommon, in fact, for a writer to be doing major scene rewrites while a show is actually being shot.

Bill Nuss:

"After someone pitches a story once, if he comes back on the same story, that meeting is free, so to speak. Once he is called for a third meeting, he technically has to be hired. The working out of the story, once he is hired, could take one, two, or three meetings."

Harlan Ellison:

"If you need two weeks, they give you ten days. If you need ten days, they give you a week. If you need a week, they need it tomorrow. They do not want it good; they want it Thursday. If you ever lose sight of that, you are losing sight of the pragmatic reality in Hollywood.

"You cannot beat this system. You've got to be prepared to bastardize yourself, and if you care about quality, you've got to be prepared to fight and not work as much as you would otherwise. It's possible to work in this town and do some good work, but things get made well more by chance than by intent."

Bob Shayne:

"They'll probably give you about a week to write the script, and by the rules of the Writers Guild minimum basic agreement they have to give you two weeks. So, if they say they need it in a week, and you want two weeks, don't be shy about it. Be polite, but don't be shy. Say you really need two weeks and turn it in in two weeks. Do be on time. It drives producers crazy when they can't depend on writers to be on time."

The point is simple. You must be able to write well and write quickly. The basic truth stated earlier appears again. To write for television you must write constantly and get yourself to the point where you write quickly, easily (well, relatively easily), and well. You get to this point by doing an enormous amount of writing. It takes practice. Writing for television is not a matter of sitting back and waiting for inspiration.

Lest you think there is something ignoble or degrading in writing quickly and to deadline, remember that Will Shakespeare was quite accustomed to writing quickly to meet the deadlines for new seasons at the Globe. Will was also used to writing roles for particular actors and for working within established genres, including the historical epic, the comedy, and even the murder mystery.

As for inspiration and the quality of your work, there doesn't really seem to be a great deal of correlation between quality in writing and the amount of time it takes to produce it. Writers have taken a lifetime to produce a single rotten novel and others, including the likes of William Faulkner, have produced some of their best novels in a few weeks under deadline pressures and the need to pay the butcher.

I've also discovered from my own experience and that of other writers that inspiration is often quite unconscious. While you are doing the grocery shopping, getting the car fixed, balancing the books, or arguing with the boss, you are also working on your script or story. True, you first have to plant the idea in your conscious, but it works. What you also find, if you are a writer or will become one, is that you sit down at your machine, set the scene, and let your characters take over. Your characters—whether it's Captain Kirk, Dick Loudon, or Mary Beth Lacey—have their own voice in your imagination. Your job is to set the scene for them and record what they say and do. That is not magic. It is imagination. Every television writer has experienced it. There is simply no time to write a line and sit back and say "What will she say next?" Sometimes you do have to work like that, but when you do you know you are in trouble. Normally, you don't have the time to ask "What will she say next?'' She simply says it in your imagination, and you write it and go on with the scene. If you don't quite like what she has said, you can go back later and change it, make it better.

Turning in the Script

When you've finished the script and brought it back to the producer or story editor, various things can happen. It can be accepted as it is—a rarity. You can be asked to work on it further—a common occurrence. You can be dismissed and the script turned over to another writer—a more common occurrence. You can be dismissed and the script taken over by the regular writing staff of the series for further changes or even complete rewriting—the most common occurrence. It is not at all uncommon for a writer's name to appear on a script that has been rewritten so extensively that he hardly recognizes it as his own. I know of one case, in fact, in which a writer has won a major award for a television script on which his name appeared even though almost nothing of his version made it to the screen.

Larry Gelbart:

"Rewriting is just part of the process of writing. It takes time to get things right. There are those rare times when people do get it right the first time, or there's not time to change it and you go with something that isn't perfect.''

Garry Marshall:

"Rewriting is the key to TV.''

Garner Simmons:

"You can expect that in every case you will see some revision. I can't remember seeing a script that has gone to film the way the writer wrote it. This is in part because almost every film has a staff of some sort, and that staff justifies its revisions by shaping the material after it comes in. If you're lucky, you will wind up seeing maybe sixty to seventy-five percent of what you originally put on the paper on the screen. If you're like most writers, you're going to find probably something closer to fifty percent. If you really have a script that gets trashed, maybe it will be twenty-five percent. But you have no way of controlling that because once you turn it in it is out of your hands. They can bring anybody else in they want to rewrite it.''

If you are lucky and you get to do several scripts for a series, it is possible that you will be asked to join the staff of that series as a writer.

Garry Marshall:

"If the beginning writer shows he can rewrite, the better the chance he has for a script to be done the way he wants it and the better the chance he has to eventually get a staff job, which is what most free-lance writers want.''

The advantage of doing so, in addition to a steady income for an uncertain future, is the opportunity to write more episodes with the possibility of few revisions, the opportunity to make more day-to-day connections with network executives and fellow writers, and the opportunity to concentrate on and help shape a series while observing first-hand the role of others involved in the production process, a process the writer may eventually wish to join.

The Role of the Director in Television

In discussing the production process and decision making, I've said little—very little—about the role of the director. It is extremely rare that a television writer will become a television director. The role of the television director is significantly different from that of the film or theatrical director. A television director, unless he or she is a regular on a series, and that happens only in half-hour comedy, is brought in at the tail end of the production process.

Bill Nuss:

"In television the director is the last element to come in, whereas in movies he's much more instrumental in being brought in on the writing stage, and movies are much more director-controlled. The directors who come in to shoot television shows come and go."

Bob Shayne:

"[*A TV director*] is hired way down the line, and the economics of television being what they are, the director is liable to be the last person into the project. By being the last hired and one of the first to leave, the director has historically not had the clout in television that he has developed in movies."

Jeff Rice:

"TV is not a director's medium, especially not hour-long drama. In such, the director is a traffic cop. He's brought in a few days before the show is filmed, gets a quick look at the script, checks the sets under construction, checks the location, then shoots with one eye on the clock and one eye on the production manager (with his stopwatch and accounting sheets). There is little time for rehearsal beyond a few moments before each scene is filmed. Once filming is wrapped, the director may stick around to work with the editor on the first cut, but more likely he'll be off on another assignment as quick as his agent can line it up.

"In sitcoms the director has far more authority and input because one or two or three directors may well stick with a show for most—if not all—of its run."

A television director is, as many in the industry have observed, a hired gun, a professional who comes in when it is time to turn the finished script into a half hour, an hour, or two hours or more of film or videotape. At that point, often a week or two before production is to begin, the director is brought in and guided through his task. Often, very often, the director is shown episodes of the series and understands that his responsibility is to continue what has been done, to make his episode coincide with the episodes before it and the ones that will follow. The producer, writer and staff, and actors of the series are the ones who exercise the maximum continuing control, not the director.

Garner Simmons:

"A television director knows that he, in episodic television, has to deliver roughly seven to eight pages a day. By contrast, a feature film is shot at maybe two and a half, maybe three pages a day. Now what that means in reality is, the amount of time a director has to spend on the close-ups and on nuances and getting a shot exactly right is like night and day between television and features. So a television director comes into a project knowing that he has been given a script that is roughly fifty-four to sixty pages long for an hour show, and he knows he has seven days to shoot it in. And if he doesn't turn it in in seven days, it is going to go over budget, and they are not going to want to hire him again. Since he really would like to think he can keep doing this kind of thing again, he really breaks everybody's back to get it in on time. The people who ride hard on him are the producers. They say, 'Listen, man. These are our production problems, and you are simply one director directing one episode out of twenty-two.' The power is clearly in the person who has to oversee the twenty-two."

Before you assume that the director is insignificant, let me point out that the director's job may be the most difficult of all of those of the creative individuals on the series. Directors can't do a season of one-hour shows simply because the pressure on them is so great on a day-to-day basis that burnout is not only likely; it is inevitable. Watching a good television director meet deadlines, cope with technical problems, and handle personalities is one of the most fascinating experiences of television.

So, with some side roads and significant digressions, you have a fairly good idea of what might take place and what you might expect if you become a television writer.

13

BREAKING INTO THE INDUSTRY

There is no set way to get that first job in television, no set way to move "up" in the industry. Each writer has his or her own story. In my case, my television work has come as a result of (a) interest in me as a novelist, (b) interest in me as a screenwriter (and remember, I achieved opportunities as a screenwriter because of my relative success as a novelist), and (c) direct contacts with friends and people in television whom I have met socially or through conferences, workshops, and meetings.

Contacts are vitally important in the industry, something to be made and nurtured. These people can both sometimes help you get an agent and help you get work once you have an agent.

Bob Shayne:

"Generally, writers are hired for almost everything out of some kind of past relationship with the person doing the hiring.

"Probably the hardest part of all this is getting your material to people who (a) will read it and (b) are close enough to the seat of power to really do something to help you. That is the key, the magic question that some people never answer. And some people are very, very lucky to just fall into the right crowd, as it were.

"Getting a job working for television executives, getting a job in development, getting a job reading scripts, can be very difficult, but some people just fall into it. That can also be a way that will lead you to making a lot of contacts, to being thought of as someone whose use should be taken somewhat seriously. It leads you to getting people to read your writing. Do anything you can think of to make personal contacts. Obviously, you are better off if you can get an invitation to a party that a producer attends than if you are parking cars at that party. At the party the producer meets you as more or less his equal—at least as someone on the level of the people at the party. But if you can't do that, you are honestly better off parking cars than relying on some small-time agent."

Garry Marshall:

"It's a real crapshoot. There's no real rule. You just got to get your material into somebody's hands so they'll take it. I've hired writers from submission by agents, from the mail, a limousine chauffeur handing the script to one of my stars because his son wrote it, from people at baseball parks coming up to me and handing me scripts. We get them from all over. The writer just has to somehow get it to the producers or directors or somebody attached to the show."

Bill Nuss:

"As far as getting your work seen is concerned, it's anybody and everybody you show it to. You show it to your friend who knows a guy who knows an agent who knows somebody who sits at a desk at an agent's office who is someone who is the story editor on a show. Any way possible. A lot of the production companies have readers to screen new writers to try to develop and find the talent. It's all toward getting that first assignment. Once you've got one assignment, it's easier to find an agent because it's easier for them to sell you."

Garner Simmons:

"In terms of beginning as writer, what you want to do is be aware of, I think, virtually any kind of writing competition, anything that will bring you to the attention of someone who is in a position to help you. There's a kind of dual currency in the television industry. That is contacts and money. You need money to survive, and you may end up working strange jobs to do it, all of which are of value as a writer because you'll come into contact with people, and what you wind up writing about are people. At the same time, the contacts will get you work or will get you in to see people at times you might not otherwise be able to see."

Let's look at how some of the television writers who have contributed to this book got into the medium.

Garry Marshall:

"I started as a gag writer for nightclubs and did one-line jokes. That was in the late fifties, just about the time the sitcom was coming into being. I guess the show that most impressed me at the time was *The Phil Silvers Show*. I was all set to write for Sid Caesar because that was where television comedy was. What came to mind was Sid Caesar and *The Ed Sullivan Show*, but Bilko was what I decided to do.

"I was in New York at the time, but you couldn't do that writing in New York, so I went to Hollywood and trained. I was a half-hour writer on *The Joey Bishop Show*, *The Danny Thomas Show*, *The Dick Van Dyke Show*, and *The Lucy Show*.

"I got on these shows because I was a nightclub comedy writer, and comedy writers were passed on from one comic to another. At that time many of the nightclub comics were getting television shows. Joey Bishop was a nightclub comic whom I wrote gags for and who took over *The Tonight Show*. He took me on. When Joey Bishop got his own television series, a half-hour sitcom, he brought me in as a punch-up writer. I wasn't doing scripts. Then Danny Thomas hired me to write scripts. A lot of those half-hour sitcoms were on the same lot, Desilu. So I had access to the people who did these shows. I could pitch them stories in the commissary."

Robert Shayne:

"I got into network writing on a fluke. I was writing a local ABC morning television show on channel 70 in Los Angeles in 1971. Ralph Story and Stephanie Edwards hosted it. *Good Morning America,* though the network never admitted it, was really patterned on the Los Angeles show. I hired a writer, Eric Cohen, who had just graduated from college, to work with me on the morning show, and he had a manager who knew the assistant to the head of program development at CBS television. At the time his title was something like Director of Development for CBS Television. Today there are departments for comedy, movies, current programming, and variety, with about three or four people in each department. We got to see the lower of the two people in the department, and we pitched an idea for a college-based half-hour situation comedy.

"Our opening line of the pitch, which was Eric's idea, was, and remember this was 1971: 'If Dobie Gillis were in college today, he'd probably look more like Maynard Krebs.' That line, and the rest of the pitch, led within 24 hours to our being hired to write a network television comedy pilot even though neither of us had ever written anything for network television. I suspect the reason we got hired was that in the staff meeting the day before somebody said, 'You know what we really need? A college comedy.' The next day we walked in with exactly what they were looking for.

"So, that's how I began writing for prime-time network television. In the next couple of years Eric and I wrote four pilots, all for CBS, all half-hour comedies. In the meantime we had graduated from writing for the morning show to working on the *Johnny Carson* show."

Harlan Ellison:

"My literary agent at the time—the late Robert Mills, in New York—said, 'You're a terrific writer, and you make decent money, but you're never going to make enough money to live the way you want to live—and live a decent life—just writing books and magazines. You've got to go to Hollywood and get into movies and television.' I was very reluctant to go, and making the trip cross-country took almost literally every cent I had.

"I limped into L.A. on January 1, 1962, with exactly ten cents in my pocket. I know this sounds like Horatio Alger, but this is the God's honest truth. I called the agent in Hollywood I was referred to, on the same day I got into town, and put on a fake voice, pretending to be my own assistant. I had incredible chutzpah and the belief I could outsmart anybody in the universe. I got them to send a car for me; I was really out of gas at the time.

"When I got to the agency, I began to do the dance of the seven veils for a roomful of agents. They asked me how many scripts I had written, and I said, 'It must be a dozen or two, but I do them in my own way.' Now, I had never even *seen* a script before. They said, 'Fine. We'll set you up with some appointments.'

"And they did. The first job I got was with Alfred Hitchcock. Then the jobs kept coming. Once you get the first credential it's easy to get *other* credentials."

Garner Simmons:

"While I was a graduate student at Northwestern University, I wrote a spec script for a contest held by Twentieth Century Fox. Out of fifty or more scripts, mine was one of three selected. This got me the attention of Gordon Stulberg, then head of production at Twentieth Century Fox. Gordon was instrumental in finding me an agent. That first agent did nothing for me. Eventually, Gordon got me another agent with whom I've been ever since."

Jeff Rice:

"Around 1970 I started submitting teleplay scripts on spec and quickly discovered, while writing my first novel, that I could get nowhere without an agent because—and this proved increasingly true as time went on—most shows are 'staff written' and few if any shows, producers, or studios (and this applies to theatrical film scripts as well) will accept delivery of 'unsolicited material,' let alone read it. Plagiarism is rife here, and they are leery of lawsuits to the point of paranoia. Thus, the script must come from a licensed literary agent, preferably one known personally to them.

"I had few (if any) contacts in the industry, but a friend of mine had a friend who knew an agent and contacted him. The agent read my first novel, *The Kolchak Papers,* over the Thanksgiving weekend of 1970 and was so excited by its potential for adaptation to a telefilm that he submitted it to the network (that subsequently bought the rights to it) even before he signed me as a client."

Bill Nuss:

"My partner and I were doing stand-up comedy and performing at Northwestern—the Meeow improv show—and working with the Second City workshops and performing in clubs in Chicago. We always wanted to write for TV, so we checked it out, and most people said that the way to break in was to write a spec script for a show that we felt we could write for. We wrote two or three spec scripts—one for *Happy Days,* one for *One Day at a Time,* and one for a show called *Alice.* Someone we knew in Chicago who had seen us perform in clubs was coming to Los Angeles and got a low-level job as a programming exec and sent us around to meet certain people. We sent our sample scripts to every contact we knew, and most of them came back unread or with polite notes. Eventually, Greg Strangis at *Eight Is Enough* read our *Alice* script.

"I think he was attracted to the funny business cards we used to print up. They said 'Nuss and Dusty'—my partner's name was Dusty—and underneath it said "Unemployed Funnymen." In one corner it had 'Bill Nuss' and my phone number, and the other corner had 'Dusty Kaye' and 'phone removed.' We used to staple these to the front of the scripts, and the guy—Greg—later told us, 'Well, you write funny business cards.' They decided to give us a shot and had us come and pitch stories—many, many stories. They finally found a couple that they liked and had us start beating out outlines of stories. After many drafts of the story, seven or eight drafts, over a period of six or seven weeks, they gave us the official 'go' and technically hired us to write story option teleplays, and that was our first script."

Larry Gelbart:

"I began as a television writer . . . [as] a natural extension of my experience as a radio writer and, to some degree, a screenwriter. It was an evolutionary process. I had had some experience in broadcasting. That's all."

Now it is up to you.

If you have done what we have recommended, you should know at this point whether or not you have the ability to write a television script. However, you won't know if you have the talent until you submit your work to an agent or a producer and get to the point where your work is actually produced.

Remember, someone has to make it, and it might as well be you.

If you have the determination and the talent, a little luck, which you can help to make, this should lead to success.

INDEX

action
  character and, 131
  dialogue and, 51
  expectations and, 123–24
  feelings and thoughts shown
    through, 62–63
  problems shown through, 21
adaptation, 144–49
agents and agencies
  fee, 169
  importance of, 50, 141, 169–70,
    179
  limitations, 173–74
  material to submit to, 174
  for new writers, 172
  obtaining of, 142, 148–49,
    170–74, 198
  WGA list of, 171
animated series, scripts for, 168
assignments, working on, 190,
    191–95
audience
  for comedy, 135–38
  for network shows, 183

beats, 36–37, 38, 133
Belson, Jerry, 67
Bergson, Henri, 121
blackouts, 128
books, TV compared to, 145–48

books mentioned in text
  American Television Genres
    (Kaminsky), 129
  Body Language (Fast), 180
  Disenchanted, The (Schulberg),
    184–185
  Hercule Poirot tales (Christie), 85
  High Midnight (Kaminsky), 165
  Kolchak Papers, The (Rice), 202
  Les Misérables (Hugo), 104
  Porfiry Petrovich Rostnikov tales
    (Kaminsky), 88
  Red Chameleon (Kaminsky), 165
  Sherlock Holmes tales (Conan
    Doyle), 85, 111, 141–42
  Toby Peter tales (Kaminsky),
    87–88
  When the Dark Man Calls
    (Kaminsky), 145–47
breaking into the industry, 198–203

California, as TV center,
    191
camera directions, 58–61
Carson, L. M. "Kit," 28
cast page, 52, 56
Chandler, Raymond, 27
character
  action and, 93, 131–35
  in children's stories, 168

character (*cont.*)
  creation of, 82–93, 131–35,
    193–94
  dialogue and, 93, 95
  feelings and thoughts of, 62
  genre and, 85, 111–12, 119, 132,
    144–45
  identification with, 41–42
  importance of, 82, 94
  in police tales, 106–16
  sources of, 87–88
  story and, 23–24, 88–89
  structure and, 37
character list, 52, 56
children's programs, 167–68
Cinemax, 178
clothing symbolism, 117
collaboration, importance of, 9–10,
    11, 136–37, 179
comeback (defined), 127
comedy, 120–38
  action in, 123–25
  audience for, 135–38
  basis of, 121–22
  characters in, 85–86, 131–35
  dialogue in, 125–26
  expectations in, 122–26, 127
  genres of, 128–31
  jokes in, 125–28
  market for, 79–80
  partner for writing of, 136–37
  pilots for, 79–80, 177–78
  pitching of, 135–38
  visuals in, 123
contacts, importance of, 13–14,
    173, 198–203
conventions, 6–7, 35, 106–7, 118–19
copyright, 164–65
costs of production, writer's
    awareness of, 52–53, 143
crime and detection genre,
    subcategories of, 103, 111–12
criminals, as characters, 104,
    108–11, 115, 117

DeNiro, Robert, 24
detective
  in classical crime and detection
    tales, 111–12

  in police tales, 112, 117
  in private eye tales, 112
detective story, characters in,
    85–86, 103, 111–12, 118
dialogue
  brevity of, 51, 62–63
  character and, 95, 193–94
  comedic, 125–26
  feelings and thoughts turned into,
    147
  illusion of reality in, 96–98, 125,
    168
  importance of, 94
  presenting problems in, 21
  redundancy of, 94
  sameness of, 95
  typing of, 62–63
director, role of, 42, 46–47, 58, 59,
    195–97
dissolve (defined), 61
documentary, 151–60
Doyle, A. Conan, 85, 111, 141–42,
    180
dreams, as source of story ideas, 28
Dumas, Alexander, 141

eavesdropping, for dialogue, 97–98
editor, role of, 46–47, 58
Ellison, Harlan
  on agents, 169, 170
  on breaking into the industry,
    201–202
  on characterization, 82
  on comedy writing, 126
  on dialogue, 94
  on feedback and criticism, 15
  on pitching, 180, 201–2
  on structure, 32
  on writing assignments, 192
empathy, *see* identification
Empire Pictures, 186
exaggeration as comic device, 127
expectations, 122–26, 127, 130
experience, drawing on, 11, 21–22, 24
exposition, 133–34

family, in police tales, 116
fantasy, 21–22, 28–29
father, as character, 130

Faulkner, William, 193
feedback and criticism, 13–15
feelings, indication of, 63
file of ideas, 26–27
film
    books compared to 145–48
    characters in, 144–45
    courses in, 160
    feature, compared with made-for-
        television movie, 144–45
films mentioned in text
    Dirty Harry, 109
    Enemy Territory, 84, 186–88
    Holiday, 73
    Lethal Weapon, 109
    List of Adrian Messenger, The,
        72, 73
    Once Upon a Time in America,
        83, 149
    Psycho, 42–43
    Teacher's Pet, 73
    When the Dark Man Calls, 88,
        145
    Winter Carnival, 184–85
    Wizard of Oz, The, 45
Fitzgerald, F. Scott, 184–85
form (*see also* format; genre)
    acceptance of and deviation from,
        130–32
    of half-hour comedy, 133
    importance of, 51, 63–64
    structure and, 9–10
format (*see also* conventions;
        genre), 48–64
    examples of, 55–57
    importance of, 51, 63–64
    registration of, 166
    writer's handling of, 9
Fox Television, 178
Freud, Sigmund, 121

gags, *see* jokes
game shows, writing for, 168
Gelbart, Larry
    on agents, 169, 170, 171, 173
    on breaking into the industry,
        203
    on camera directions, 58
    on collaboration, 137

on comedy writing, 131
on format, 53, 54
on pitching, 180–81
on producer's role, 177
on rewriting, 194
on story ideas, 49
on writing schools, 11
Gennette, Gerard, 22
genre (*see also* conventions; form)
    character and, 85, 111–12, 119,
        132
    in comedy, 128–31
    defined, 64
    reasons for study of, 101, 103,
        118–19
    situation and, 132

HBO, 139–40, 178
history, *see under* story
Hollywood Reporter, 67
''hook,'' 35–36
humor (*see also* comedy)
    creation of, 86
    definition of, 121
    expectations and, 122–26
    writer's approach to, 121–22

ideas
    of beginning writers, 8, 48–49,
        67, 68, 137
    for documentaries, 151–52, 160
    file of, 26–27
    for made-for-television movies, 141–43
    for miniseries, 150
    notebook, 24–26
    professionals' views on, 48–49,
        50, 67
    protection of, 67, 163–66, 170
    sources of, 28–29
    stealing of, 50
    tape recorder for, 29
    use of other people's, 27
identification, 41–47
    devices for control of, 43–47
    by viewer, 41
    by writer, 41–42, 46–47, 87
imagination (*see also* fantasy), 12,
        87, 193
inspiration, role of, 193

jokes
    classification of, 127–28
    counting of, 126
    exposition through, 133, 135
    frequency of, 126
    Freud's theory of, 121
    juxtaposition of ideas, 127
    market for, 168–69
    pitching of, 136
    types of, 126–27
    verbal, 127
    visual (sight gags), 123

language, control of, 12–13
local shows
    pitching comedy on, 138
    writing for, 169
location
    choice of, 143, 145
    indication of, 52, 57, 61
Los Angeles, as TV center, 191

made-for television movies, 139–49
    adaptations for, 140–41, 144–49
    feature films compared with, 144
    ideas for, 141–43
    pilots for, 80, 177–78
    pitching of, 183
    proposal for, 72–79
    ratings of, 140
    script for, 143–48
    treatment for, 38–40
market
    for children's programs, 167–68
    for documentaries, 159
    finding of, 166–69
    for first novels, 148–49
    for game show material, 168
    for half-hour comedies, 79–80
    for jokes, 168–69
    for made-for-television movie
        scripts, 149
    for miniseries, 149
    for novels adaptable for
        television, 149
    for quiz show material, 168
    for specials, 168–69
    for talk show material, 128–29, 168–69
    for variety show material, 128, 168–69

Marshall, Garry
    on agents, 173
    on breaking into the industry,
        199, 200
    on camera directions, 59
    on collaboration, 136
    on dialogue, 95
    on differences among production
        companies, 132–33
    on format, 53
    on frustration, 14
    on likability of characters, 134
    on made-for-TV movies, 144
    on pitching, 136, 181
    on producer's role, 177
    on rewriting, 194, 195
    on spec scripts, 67
    on story ideas, 49
    on structure, 31
    on writing schools, 11
melodrama, police tale compared
    with, 103
minseries, 149–50
    adaptations for, 140–41, 144–49
    ideas for, 150
    market for, 149
    pilots for, 177
    preparing script for, 150
    treatment for, 38–40, 149–50
movie-of-the-week, *see* made-for-
    television movie
movie, feature, *see* film; films
mystery
    police genre compared to, 103
    sample proposal for, 72–79

narrative comedy, 129–38
narrator, 43–45
networks, getting readings by, 50,
    175–79
news, as source of ideas, 26–27,
    142–43
New York, as television center,
    191
notebook
    for dialogue, 97–99
    for story ideas, 24–27
    for TV watching, 29, 36, 132
    for writing done, 3

novel
    adaptation of, 148
    writing of, as entrée to
        television, 148, 198, 202
Nuss, Bill
    on breaking into the industry,
        199, 202–3
    on camera directions, 58
    on collaboration, 136, 137
    on dialogue, 94
    on director's role, 196
    on format, 53
    on made-for-TV movies, 144–45
    on pitching, 181
    on producers, 176
    on spec scripts, 65
    on story ideas, 49
    on structure, 30
    on writing assignments, 192
    on writing schools, 11

one-liner (defined), 127
opening sequence, 134
option, adaptation, 140–41
outline, 38, 166

pace, 36
partner, see collaboration
payment, importance of, 184
perception, as identification device,
    45
pilots, 79–80, 139–40, 177–78
Pinkerton, Alan, 105
pitching, 179–91
    of comedy, 136–38
    defined, 179–80, 183
    of documentaries, 159
    importance of, 180–85
    technique of, 183–91, 201–2
point of view, 45–46
police tale, 103–19
    automobile symbol in, 117–18
    characters in, 106–16
    clothing symbol in, 117
    criminals in, 108–11, 115
    family life in, 116
    gun symbol in, 117
    illusion of reality in, 105–6
    informers in, 115

kinds of, 106
    mythology of, 108–11
    order and individualism in, 111
    origins of, 104–6
    police in, 106–8
    as potential tragedy, 118
    private detective tale compared
        with, 103, 112, 118
    settings and locations of, 116
    social class in, 111–12, 115–16,
        117
    structure of, 112–14
posters, as source of ideas, 26
practice, importance of, 3, 29, 121,
    193
pressure, writing under, 8, 67, 179,
    190–95
private detective tale
    police tale compared with, 103,
        112, 118
    series proposal for, 69–72
problem (see also story)
    exposition as, 133
    primary and secondary, 17–19,
        21, 35–36, 107, 133
producers
    getting material to, 172, 175–79
    location of, 191
    pitching comedy to, 136
production, training in, 160
production companies
    differences among, 132–33, 133
    getting readings by, 50
production process, 178–79, 191,
    195
production value, 52–53
projection
    by viewer, 41–42, 135
    by writer, 87
proposal, 68–81, 186–88
public domain
    plays and novels in, 140, 141–42
    public figures in, 142
public figures, as subjects, 142, 152

quiz shows, material for, 168

Rashomon gimmick, 44
reality, illusion of, 23–24

repetition, as structural device, 36–37
research, 28–29, 149, 150
rewriting, 14, 67, 179, 191, 192, 194–95
Rice, Jeff
  on breaking into the industry, 202
  on camera directions, 59
  on director's role, 196
  on made-for-TV movies, 145
  on pitching, 181–82
  on producer's role, 176
  on spec scripts, 64
rich people
  in classical crime and detection tales, 111–12
  in police tales, 115–16
rights, adaptation, 140–41
romances, characters in, 85–86

scene
  as element in story, 21, 29
  imagining of, 85
  as structural element, 38
  study of, 29
  writing of, 95
Schulberg, Budd, 184–85
science fiction, police tale compared with, 103
screenwriting, as entrée to television writing, 198, 203
scripts (see also spec scripts)
  form of, see format
  getting readings of, 50
  length of, 32–36
  protection of, 163–66, 170
  quantity of, 191, 192–93
  registration of, 166
  revision of, 14, 67, 179, 191–95
  sample pages of, 55, 56, 57, 60
  unsolicited, 50, 170, 172–73
Shakespeare, William, 27, 141, 193
Shayne, Bob
  on agents, 172, 174
  on breaking into the industry, 198–199, 200–201
  on collaboration, 136, 137

  on director's role, 196
  on format, 54
  on free-lancing, 14
  on made-for-TV movies, 145
  on pitching, 182
  on producers, 176
  on spec scripts, 65, 67
  on story ideas, 49
  on structure, 32
  on writing assignments, 192
Sherlock Holmes stories, 85, 111, 141–42, 180
Showtime, 139–40, 178
sight gags, 123
Simmons, Garner
  on agents, 169, 170, 172
  on breaking into the industry, 199–200, 202
  on camera directions, 59
  on creating illusion of reality, 24
  on difference between novel and TV writing, 148
  on director's role, 197
  on format, 54
  on forms, 9
  on pitching, 182–83
  on producers, 176
  on revising, 194–95
  on spec scripts, 65, 66
  on script length, 33–34
  on stealing of ideas, 164
  on structure, 30–31
sitcoms, see comedy
situation
  character and, 131–35
  genre and, 132
sketches, 128
social class
  in detective genres, 111–12
  in police tales, 112, 115–16, 117
  of television viewers, 112
specials, writing for, 168
spec scripts, 64–68
  characters in, 82, 132
  defined, 64
  for half-hour comedy, 135
  for made-for-television movie, 140–50
  for narrative comedy, 129

spec scripts (*cont.*)
  pitching of, 183
  purpose of, 64–68, 179, 190
speed of writing, 67
spin-off series, ideas for, 29
staff writer, 179, 191, 194, 195
stand-up material, 128
stinger, 36, 127, 133
stopwatch, for TV study, 36, 132
story (*see also* structure), 17–29
  character and, 23–24, 88–89
  for children, 68
  elements of, 19–22
  history and, 22–23, 29
  ideas for, 24–29
  problem as element in, *see*
    problem
  registration of, 166
  relative importance of, 94
  research for, 28–29
  steps for converting into
    television episode, 21
structure (*see also* story), 30–47
  by acts, 34–36
  character as element of, 37
  defined, 30–32
  identification and, 41–47
  importance of, 9, 31–32
  length of script and, 32–36
  outline of, 38
  pacing as element of, 36–37
  of police show, 112–14
  problem as element in, 35–36
  of scenes, 38
  situation and, 135
  treatment outline, 38–40
  summary, 69–70
syndication, 178–79
synopsis, 166

talent nights, pitching on, 138
talent, development of, 10–12,
  120–121
talk show, writing for, 128–29, 168
tape recorder, for story ideas, 29
television shows mentioned in text
  Adam 12, 106
  ALF, 43, 126, 134
  All in the Family, 125

Amerika, 150
Basic Training, 157
Beverly Hillbillies, The, 123, 134
Buck James, 5
Cagney and Lacey, 27, 51, 103
Centennial, 150
Cheers, 65, 130, 132
Chiefs, 150
CHiPs, 106
Columbo, 106
Cosby Show, The, 130, 132
Crime Story, 103, 106
Designing Women, 132
Dick Van Dyke Show, The, 123
Dolly, 128
Dragnet, 105
Duet, 130
Ed Sullivan Show, The, 128
Equalizer, The, 18–19, 66
Family Ties, 131
Fatal Vision, 150
Father Knows Best, 130
Fridays, 128
Fugitive, The, 104–5
Gangster Chronicles, The, 104
Green Acres, 134
Happy Days, 126
Head of the Class, 130, 132, 134
Helter Skelter, 150
High School, 157
Highway Patrol, 105
Hill Street Blues, 103, 106
Honeymooners, The, 35–36, 123,
  129
Hunter, 103, 106
I Love Lucy, 36, 123, 123–24,
  126, 129
Kate and Allie, 43
Late Night with David Letterman,
  129
Late Show, The, 129
Laverne and Shirley, 65, 134
Law and Order, 157
Leave It to Beaver, 132
Magnum, P.I., 34–35, 37–38,
  43, 103
Married: With Children, 132
Martian Chronicles, The, 150
Mary Tyler Moore, 125

television shows mentioned in text (*cont.*)
  M*A*S*H, 43, 51, 125, 130
  Maverick, 125
  Miami Vice, 103
  Mike Hammer, 43, 103, 112
  Milton Berle Show, The, 128
  Missiles of October, The, 150
  Moonlighting, 45, 103, 107
  M Squad, 105
  Muppet Babies, The, 45
  Murder, She Wrote, 85, 111
  Newhart, 29, 134
  Night Court, 65
  North and South, 150
  Odd Couple, The, 134
  Once Upon a Time in America,
    149–150
  Our Father's House (proposed
    miniseries), 39–40
  Overboard, 5
  Perfect Strangers, 126
  Racket Squad, 105
  Remington Steele, 107
  Rhoda, 130
  Rocky King, 105
  Roots, 150
  Saturday Night Live, 124–25,
    128
  Scarecrow and Mrs. King, 66
  Second City Television, 128
  Shepard's Tower, 149
  Simon and Simon, 103, 107
  60 Minutes, 151
  Sledge Hammer, 103, 105, 106
  Space, 150
  Spenser: For Hire, 5, 66, 103,
    112, 148
  T. J. Hooker, 106
  Tonight Show, The, 129
  Tracy Ullman Show, The, 128
  20/20, 151
  Twilight Zone, The, 44
  Untouchables, The, 24, 104
  V, 150
  Valerie, 18
  *Washington Behind Closed
    Doors*, 150
  WKRP in Cincinnati, 132
  Woman in the Wind, A, 83–84
television watching, with eye of
  writer, 29, 36, 132, 143
tempo, 36
thriller
  characters in, 85–86
  police tale compared with, 103
title, rights to, 165
title page, 52, 55
Toronto, as television center, 191
tragedy
  characters in, 85–86
  police tale and, 118
treatment, 21, 38–40, 148, 149–50

unsolicited scripts, 50, 170,
  172–73
USA network, 178

Vancouver, as television center,
  191
Variety, 67, 149
variety show, 128–29, 168
video-making courses, 160
voice-over narrator, 43–45

western, police tale and, 107
"What If?" 28–29
Wiseman, Frederick, 157
witticism (defined), 127
Writers Guild of America
  agency list, 171
  membership requirements, 166–67
  Newsletter, 167
  Registration Service, 50, 165–66
writing courses
  attributes of, 11
  for getting readings of script, 50
  for making contacts with
    professionals, 173
  pitching comedy at, 138
  what to look for in, 13

STUART M. KAMINSKY has written and continues to write for television, film, and print. He is the author of more than twenty-five novels and works of nonfiction, including the Toby Peters mystery series, the Porfiry Petrovich Rostnikov series (the second of which was an Edgar Allan Poe Award nominee), and *When the Dark Man Calls*, which was recently filmed in France starring Catherine Deneuve. His film credits include dialogue for *Once Upon a Time in America,* which starred Robert De Niro and James Woods; and story and co-screenplay for *Enemy Territory,* which starred Gary Frank, Ray Parker, Jr., and Jan-Michael Vincent. His television credits range from CBS-TV's Repertoire Workshop to a soon-to-be-released movie for television, *A Woman in the Wind,* which stars Colleen Dewhurst and Jay O. Sanders. He is under contract to write a comedy-mystery for MGM, and has a made-for-television movie, *Shepard's Tower,* under option. Kaminsky holds a B.S. in Journalism and an M.A. in English Literature from the University of Illinois, in addition to a Ph.D. in Speech from Northwestern University, where he has taught film and television writing for more than ten years. He is Chairman of the Department of Radio/Television/Film at Northwestern, where he also heads the Program in Creative Writing for the Media. Kaminsky lives in Skokie, Illinois, with his wife, Enid, and his children.

MARK WALKER has taught comedy writing and holds a Ph.D. from Northwestern University.